Pennsylvania's Scenic Route 6

A Guide to Historic Sites, Towns and Natural Lands

Pennsylvania's Scenic Route 6
A Guide to Historic Sites, Towns and Natural Lands
Text © 2002 by John G. Hope
Photography © 2002 by Blair Seitz
ISBN 1-879441-86-1

Library of Congress Control Number 2002 190005

All rights reserved. No part of this book may be reproduced or transmitted in any form or by any means, electronic or mechanical, including photocopying, recording or by any information storage or retrieval system without written permission from the author, except for inclusion of brief quotations in a review.

Seitz & Seitz, Inc.
1010 North Third Street
Harrisburg, PA 17102
www.celebratePA.com

Designed by Klinginsmith & Company

Printed in China by Regent Publishing Services

Pennsylvania's Scenic Route 6
A Guide to Historic Sites, Towns and Natural Lands

I·N·S·I·G·H·T·S

Published by

RB BOOKS

Harrisburg, PA

John G. Hope

Photography by Blair Seitz

Page 1: The Knox & Kane Railroad takes visitors on a 96-mile trip through the peaks and valleys of the Allegheny National Forest to the 301-foot-high Kinzua Bridge, the second-highest railroad viaduct in the United States and fourth-highest in the world. **Pages 2-3:** Much of U.S. Route 6 in Pennsylvania is a two-lane highway.

Foreword

It is a real pleasure to be associated with this book on U.S. Route 6 in Pennsylvania. My family moved to Mansfield in Tioga County in 1937, when I was less than a year old. Between 1938 and 1940 we lived in a house on Cole Street, just a block north of Route 6—which was then called the Roosevelt Highway—and a roll of color movie film that my father took shows me in the snow near our house, with a shield-shaped U.S. 6 route marker plainly visible behind me!

During the remainder of my years in Mansfield we lived closer to the northern end of town, but I remember that my walk to elementary school took me past the college campus along Sullivan Street—a part of Route 6—and I also remember the many times as a boy that I found myself admiring the U.S. 6 and U.S. 15 route markers that were at the square right in the center of Mansfield.

At that time I did not know how unusual it was for two such highways to intersect in a town with a 1940 census population of 1,880, nor did I know that U.S. 6 was then the nation's longest transcontinental highway—longer than the Lincoln Highway, U.S. 30—extending all the way from Provincetown, Massachusetts, to Long Beach, California. Even today, some 60 years later, Route 6 still covers most of the territory that it did then—ending now at Bishop in eastern California—and, especially in Pennsylvania, this picturesque highway is relatively unchanged from what it was six decades ago. While many of this state's other major highways have been transformed or replaced during the intervening years, the sparsely settled territory through which much of U.S. 6 passes has enabled it to retain a surprising amount of its historic character.

Having been involved with the marker program at the Pennsylvania Historical and Museum Commission since 1977, when I was named the program's coordinator, I am aware of the many historical markers that have been erected on or close to U.S. 6 over the years.

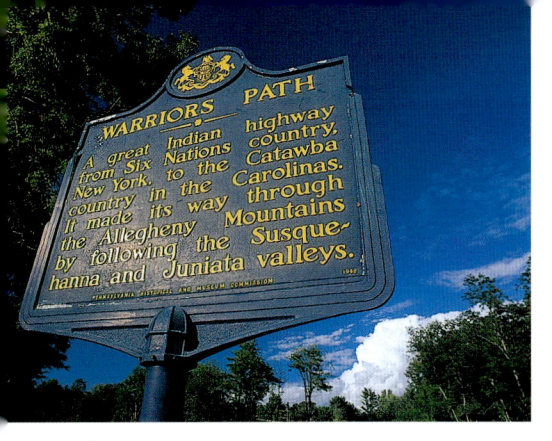

In 1946, the Pennsylvania Historical and Museum Commission began placing blue and gold markers to mark sites of historical significance, including this one in Wyalusing describing the Warriors Path Indian trail.

This includes markers at 10 county courthouses in northern Pennsylvania placed in observance of the Commonwealth's tercentenary in 1981 and 1982. Another marker—a favorite of mine—honors the Civilian Conservation Corps and is at Leonard Harrison State Park overlooking Pennsylvania's Grand Canyon; its dedication was attended by a large and happy group of CCC alumni and their families in 1995. Still another marker, commemorating the forester and governor Gifford Pinchot and detailing his career, was dedicated just off Route 6 near Milford in 2000.

In all, there are close to 90 historical markers on U.S. 6 or in its vicinity in the 11 Pennsylvania counties through which this highway passes. (The highway goes through or close to the county seat of each of these 11 counties except Erie.) These markers are among the more than 1,800 that are described in the newest *Guide to the State Historical Markers of Pennsylvania* published at the end of 2000 by the Pennsylvania Historical and Museum Commission.

As I retire from my duties at the commission, I look back at the more than 40 years since I originally joined the staff in 1961. I also look back at the relationships that I have formed outside the PHMC, including my long and continuing friendship with both Blair Seitz and John Hope. In the light of that friendship, I feel privileged to be able to contribute to their fine book and am happy to commend it to you, the reading public.

George Redman Beyer

Introduction

I've always enjoyed traveling, especially by car, but the research for this book went far beyond enjoyment to an almost magical and mystical experience. My wife, Anna, and I live in Harrisburg and appreciate our home and neighborhood very much. The state's capital is surrounded by Interstate highways that we put to good use in getting around for work, shopping, and pleasure. Because I grew up in Philadelphia and went to graduate school in Pittsburgh, Harrisburg still feels like a small town to me, and there are many things about it that I really value.

But I must admit I came to look forward to escaping from home north on Interstate 81 or U.S. 15 to U.S. 6. The first couple of times I made the trip, I could almost feel a physical change come over me as I turned onto that highway. I could feel cares and stress fall away as I reveled in the beauty of my surroundings. On later trips, I expected that change to occur and never was disappointed. And when Anna joined me, she felt the same sense of peace and calm.

Although it is a U.S. highway, much of U.S. 6 is two or three lanes, with a speed limit of 55 m.p.h. There's not a lot of traffic, meaning you can drive it without the intense concentration and sometimes fear that is part of modern Interstate highway driving. And for much of the 400 miles from New Jersey in the east to Ohio in the west, the vista alternates between beautiful forested areas and quaint small towns with old Victorian homes. It really doesn't get much better than this.

My notebook reminds me of things that struck me on my trips to the area:

- *a small wooden church with its doors open for natural air conditioning on a pleasant summer Sunday morning;*

- *the placemat in Stewart's Family Restaurant in Towanda advertising a local Methodist Church's Family Night with dinner at the restaurant and a showing of the movie "The Secret Garden" at the local movie theater, all for an extraordinarily low price;*
- *the sign welcoming visitors to New Albany, founded "a long time ago";*
- *the description of Wysox as "a golden mile";*
- *running into a traffic jam in Towanda, not where I'd expected to find one;*
- *driving between Towanda and Troy and given an opportunity to really appreciate the beauty of the scenery as I had to stay behind a slow-moving tractor-trailer;*
- *bunting on gas street lights in Wellsboro and American flags on parking meters, long before the renewed patriotism that followed September 11, 2001;*
- *weathered but proud American flags on utility poles in Newfoundland, again well before September 11;*
- *the shopping center (according to the sign) that consisted of four old shacks;*
- *occasional glimpses of Lake Wallenpaupack, the state's third largest lake;*
- *all the rabbits running around Foote Rest campground;*
- *breakfast at Don and Marsha's Restaurant in Mt. Jewett, where the waitress seemed surprised when I ordered the Logger's Breakfast and questioned whether I would be able to finish it. Her concern stemmed from the fact that the breakfast is delivered on two large plates, one covered with eggs, sausage, toast, and homefries, and the other containing two thick pancakes that are as big as the plate itself. (The waitress' concern was well-placed, although I ate more than I ever thought I would.)*
- *Large statues of whimsical fish all over downtown Erie and large statues of black bears in various poses during a special celebration at Milford.*

We've talked with people who live in the area and swear it is every bit as charming, friendly, and wonderful as it seems to those who visit. I hope you'll travel U.S. Route 6 and experience the same wonderful feelings we had.

John Hope
HARRISBURG, PENNSYLVANIA

PRESQUE ISLE STATE PARK

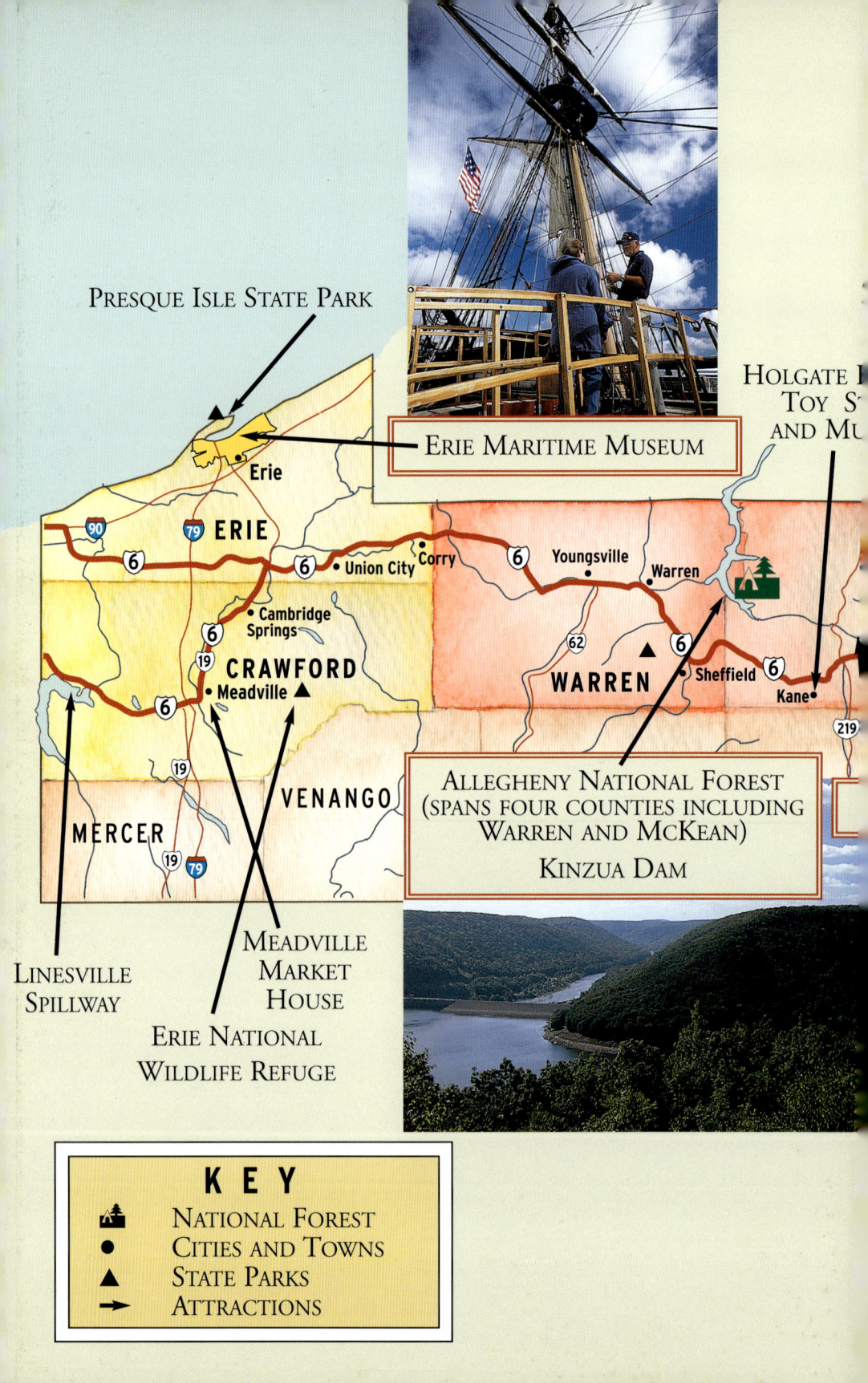

ERIE MARITIME MUSEUM

HOLGATE
TOY S
AND MU

- Erie
- Union City
- Corry
- Youngsville
- Warren
- Cambridge Springs
- Meadville
- Sheffield
- Kane

ERIE · **CRAWFORD** · **VENANGO** · **MERCER** · **WARREN**

ALLEGHENY NATIONAL FOREST
(SPANS FOUR COUNTIES INCLUDING WARREN AND McKEAN)
KINZUA DAM

LINESVILLE SPILLWAY

MEADVILLE MARKET HOUSE

ERIE NATIONAL WILDLIFE REFUGE

KEY
- 🌲 NATIONAL FOREST
- ● CITIES AND TOWNS
- ▲ STATE PARKS
- → ATTRACTIONS

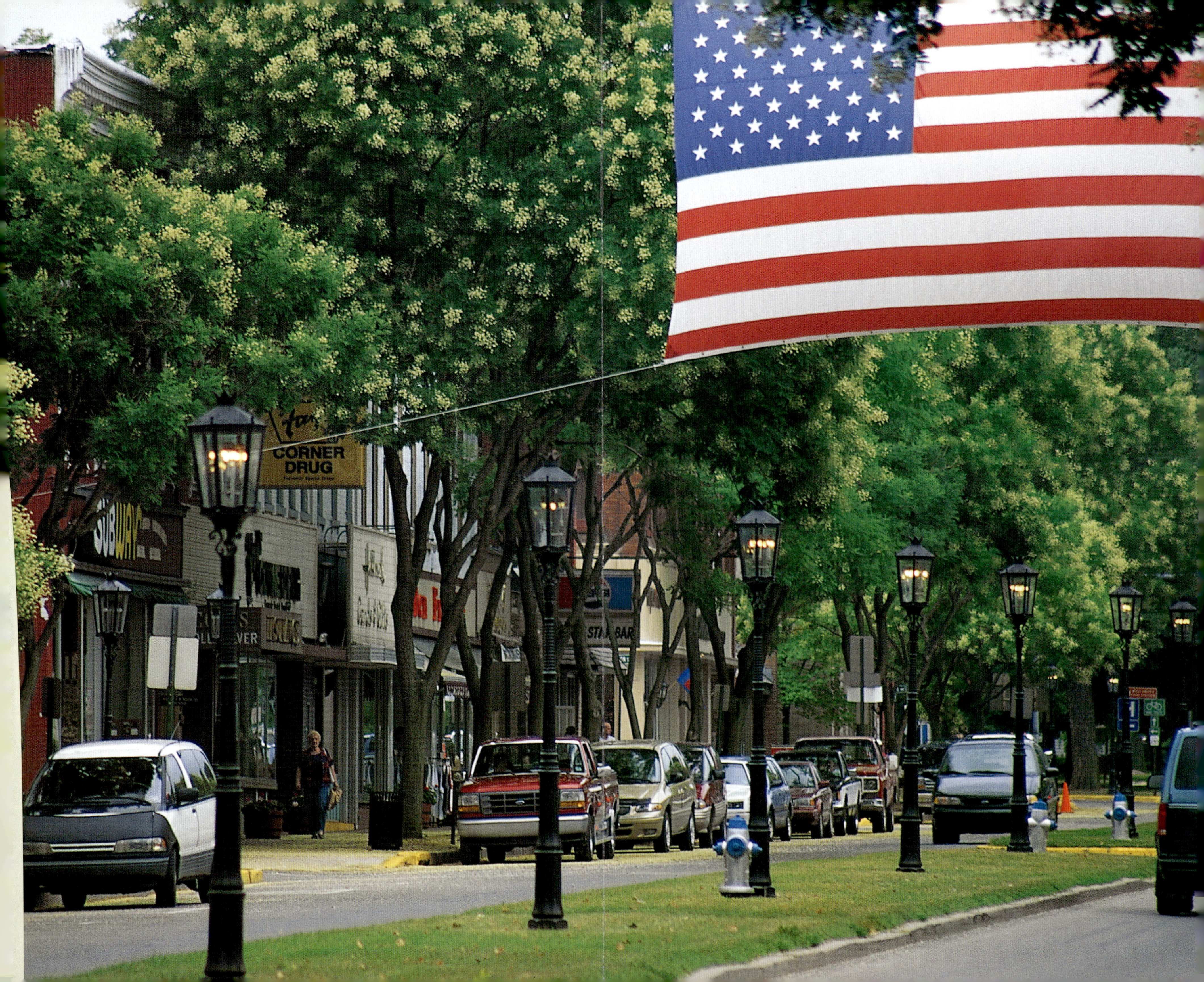

CORNER
DRUG
SUBWAY

Map of Northern Pennsylvania Along Route 6

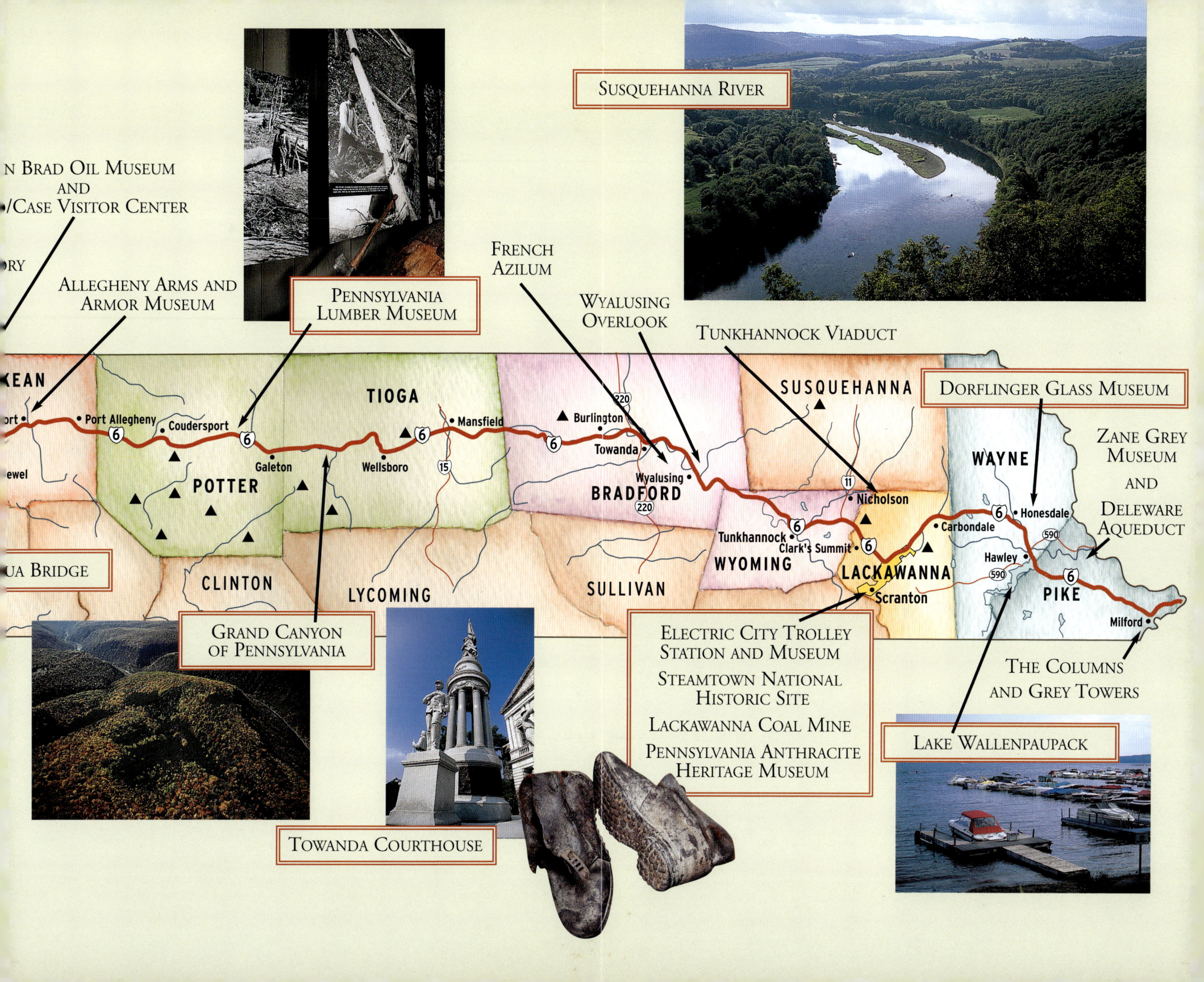

Counties shown (west to east): McKean, Potter, Tioga, Clinton, Lycoming, Bradford, Sullivan, Susquehanna, Wyoming, Lackawanna, Wayne, Pike

Towns shown: Port Allegheny, Coudersport, Galeton, Wellsboro, Mansfield, Burlington, Towanda, Wyalusing, Tunkhannock, Nicholson, Clark's Summit, Scranton, Carbondale, Honesdale, Hawley, Milford

Points of Interest

- Brad Oil Museum and /Case Visitor Center
- Allegheny Arms and Armor Museum
- Pennsylvania Lumber Museum
- Susquehanna River
- French Azilum
- Wyalusing Overlook
- Tunkhannock Viaduct
- Dorflinger Glass Museum
- Zane Grey Museum and Deleware Aqueduct
- Grand Canyon of Pennsylvania
- Towanda Courthouse
- Electric City Trolley Station and Museum
- Steamtown National Historic Site
- Lackawanna Coal Mine
- Pennsylvania Anthracite Heritage Museum
- The Columns and Grey Towers
- Lake Wallenpaupack

A Concrete Tribute
to TR and the GAR

In the beginning, of course, it was Indian trails. Much of what was originally Pennsylvania Route 7 and is now U.S. Route 6 follows trails laid out by the Indians who were in the northern tier of Pennsylvania long before white men and their motor cars.

The 1929 edition of *Pennsylvania Highways* notes that the section of highway from Larabee to Coudersport followed a part of the "Forbidden Path," while the section from Towanda to Milford ran almost exactly over the Indian trail taken by Sullivan's Army in 1779.

At the time that it was known as Pennsylvania Route 7, and in the early days of U.S. Route 6, it was nicknamed the Roosevelt Highway in honor of President Theodore Roosevelt.

As our national highway system evolved in the late 1920s, the road that ultimately traveled coast-to-coast for more than 3,500 miles began in Provincetown, Massachusetts, on the tip of Cape Cod, and proceeded off cape and then across the southern shore of Massachusetts. It entered Rhode Island, passed through Providence, and then cut Connecticut in half and on to Brewster, New York. It continued west-southwest through New York and into Pennsylvania, ending at Erie.

In 1933, the connection to Erie was cut when the road was moved further south to Edinboro and then still further south to Meadville in 1938. (There is now a 6N that brings the highway back close to Erie.) In 1933, also, the western terminus was Greeley, Colorado.

In 1938, the Sons of Union Veterans of the Civil War led the drive to have U.S. Route 6, now going all the way to Long Beach, California, declared The Grand Army of the Republic Highway. A joint resolution in the U.S. House of Representatives adopted in 1937 called on all states through which the highway ran to name it in honor of the Grand Army of the Republic and sign it accordingly.

Today, in Pennsylvania, it is possible to see both GAR Highway and Roosevelt Highway signs, as well as a sign on one spur honoring former Gov. Robert P. Casey.

Table of Contents

Northern Poconos 14

Lackawanna County 38

Endless Mountains 55

Potter and Tioga Counties 76

Allegheny National Forest Region 93

Erie Region 116

Previous Pages: Arguably the quaintest town in a quaint region, **Wellsboro** has gas lights lining the main streets and a profuse display of American flags, giving tourists an impression of a 19th century New England town, understandable since New England colonists founded it in 1806.

Right: Fall colors delight the eye in this aerial shot **between Milford and Lake Wallenpaupack.**

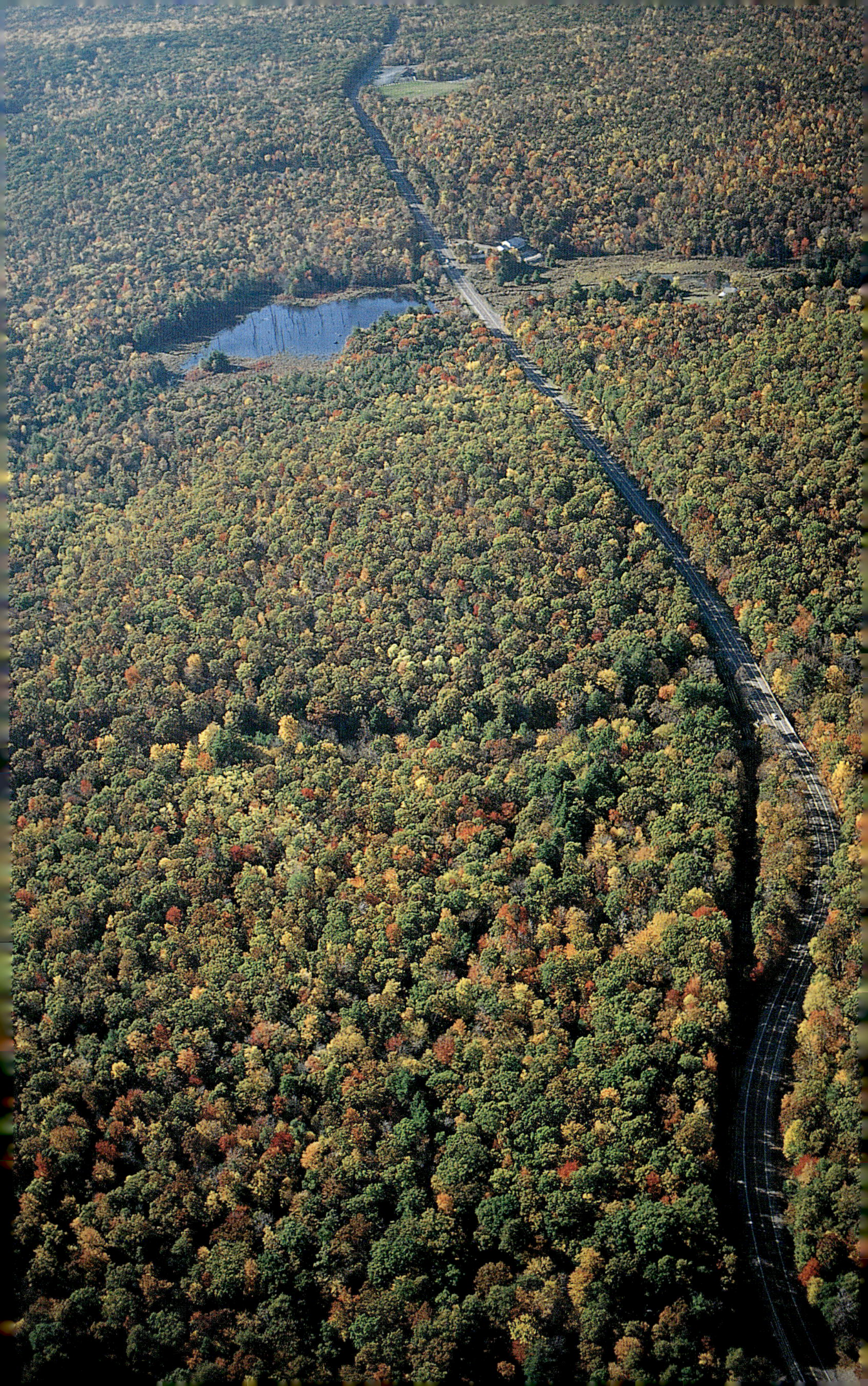

Northern Poconos

THE COLUMNS

One of the most picturesque and interesting towns along U.S. Route 6 is Milford, at the eastern end of the highway, across the river from New Jersey. I had gone there myself to do research for this book and then went back again with my wife, Anna, because I knew she would like the New Hope, Bucks County, feel of the town.

One of the main attractions for visitors to Milford is The Columns, the museum of the Pike County Historical Society. The neo-classical mansion on Broad Street houses a diverse collection of art and artifacts.

One of the most impressive items is a large American flag that reportedly had been draped at the box at Ford's Theatre in Washington in which Abraham Lincoln was sitting when he was shot by John Wilkes Booth. The flag had been placed under the dying president's head by Thomas Gourlay, a part-time stage manager at the theatre. Gourlay retrieved the flag after Lincoln was taken from the theatre and later gave it to his daughter, Jeannie Gourlay Struthers, who ultimately settled in Pike County. She passed the flag on to her son, who donated it to the Pike County Historical Society in 1954.

Museum officials say that extensive research testing on the flag and its blood stains, as well as the written chain of ownership detailed by the

---

The **DORFLINGER-SUYDAM WILDLIFE SANCTUARY** offers walking trails and scenic vistas on 600 acres around the Dorflinger Glass Museum. The Wildflower Festival of Music & Art is held on the grounds each summer.

Following the September 2001 terrorist attacks in New York City and Washington, D.C., American flags were much in evidence along U.S. Route 6 and throughout the country. Here flags are displayed on Milford's Guliak/Hoagland house dating from 1865, and the 1845 Davis P. Chant Realtor and Cornelius Bull law office now occupied by the Pike County Chamber of Commerce.

family when the flag was given to the historical society, have confirmed the flag's authenticity.

Other exhibits at The Columns describe the work of Charles Sanders Pierce, a scientist and mathematician and founder of the philosophy of pragmatism; Chief Thundercloud, the face on the last $5 gold piece minted in the U.S., and Gifford Pinchot, conservationist and a governor of Pennsylvania (whose estate, Grey Towers, is operated by the USDA Forest Service in Milford).

The stagecoach Hiawatha is given a prominent display alongside the main museum building, and there are collections of 18th and 19th century clothing, medical instruments, and other memorabilia from the county.

VISITORS INFORMATION: The Columns is at 608 Broad Street, Milford. Telephone: (570) 296-8126.

Pike County artifacts and historical memorabilia are displayed at The Columns, the county's historical museum in Milford.

Grey Towers

The Grey Towers mansion in Milford, the home in which legendary Pennsylvania governor and conservationist Gifford Pinchot first decided to pursue forestry as a career, is now operated by the United States Department of Agriculture's Forest Service as a national historic landmark.

Grey Towers was designed by Richard Morris Hunt as a summer mansion for the James Pinchot family in 1886, and was intended to reflect the family's French heritage. For two decades around 1900, the family and their children spent summers at Grey Towers, entertaining guests for afternoon teas, dinner parties, and outdoor activities.

When Gifford Pinchot's interests moved from conservation to politics, Grey Towers became his legal residence. Shortly after, he married Cornelia Bryce, who undertook a redesign of the interior, furnishings, and landscape at the mansion. She enlarged the library, added furnishings, created a sitting room, and moved the dining room outdoors, all intended to create a modern home more suited to their active lifestyle.

Grey Towers is now a conference center for conservation issues and the operational headquarters for the Pinchot Institute for Conservation. It was reopened to the public late in 2001 after undergoing portions of a significant restoration and rehabilitation. The entire restoration is projected to cost $18 million. The latest phase involved additional visitor parking, increased educational facilities and services, construction of a visitor pavilion, improved walkways and lighting, restoration of a historic carriage road, and an improved walkway between the parking area and amphitheater.

The mansion is open for tours from Memorial Day to Labor Day, and by appointment the rest of the year.

VISITORS INFORMATION: Grey Towers is outside of Milford. Follow signs. Telephone (570) 296-9630. www.pinchot.com

Conservationist and former Pennsylvania Gov. Gifford Pinchot, who once said that he would like to come back after 100 years to see the trees at his Pike County estate, Grey Towers, would be pleased indeed. Now operated by the U.S. Forest Service as a conservation and education center, Grey Towers was Pinchot's family home and political base.

Gifford Pinchot's wife, Cornelia, first thought of Grey Towers as a dreary castle standing naked on a hill. Using much of her own money, she decided to "jazz it up." Her exterior remodeling included additional gardens, an outdoor dining area with a unique water table, a partial moat, an elaborate playhouse for their son, and an office for Gifford called the Letterbox. Inside the mansion, she combined rooms, added windows, and redecorated extensively.

The Upper Delaware Scenic and Recreational River is 73.4 miles of free-flowing stream that is enjoyed by thousands of people yearly. The best way to see and truly get to know the area is from the river itself aboard a canoe, kayak, raft, or even inner tube. Most of the area is rated Class I, meaning there are few obstructions or problems for novice boaters. It also is a popular fishing stream for brown and rainbow trout, smallmouth bass, walleye, white suckers, fallfish, and American eels.

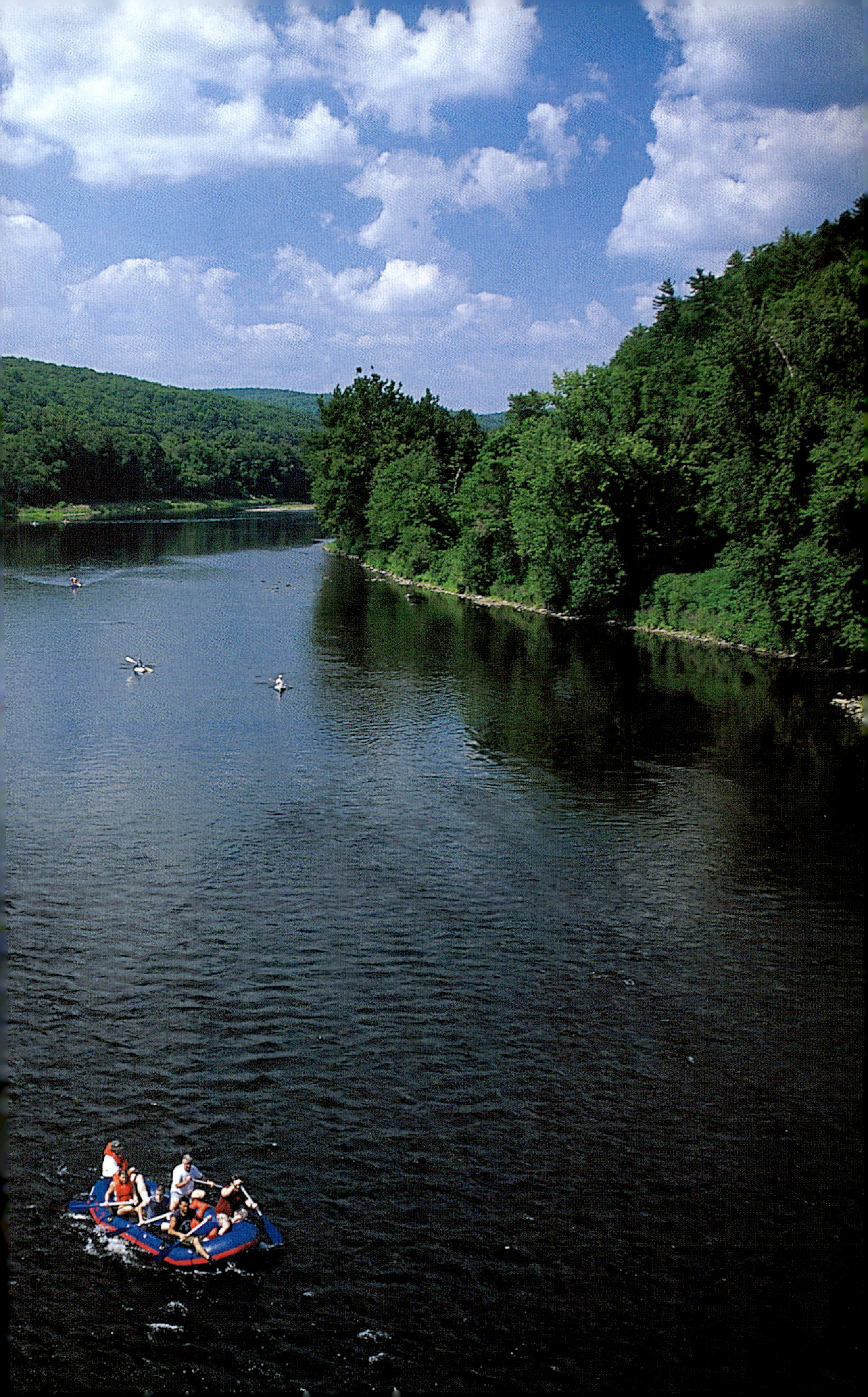

Delaware Aqueduct

The Delaware Aqueduct, now also known as the Roebling Bridge, is the oldest existing wire suspension bridge in the United States. It was a beautiful, sunny fall day when I traveled to Lackawaxen to see the bridge and tour the Zane Grey Museum. I parked at the Pennsylvania end of the bridge and walked across into New York State, stopping in the middle to look at the beauty of the upper Delaware River and watch as some boaters passed in canoes and kayaks.

The old tollbooth on the New York side of the bridge contains photos and exhibits about the need for the bridge and its construction, and about Roebling. The bridge was built because of conflicts between two local industries—coal mining and timbering. Anthracite coal from northeastern Pennsylvania was taken to New York City by way of the Delaware & Hudson Canal, which had been built in the 1820s. And timber from the valley was floated down the Delaware River to Trenton, New Jersey, and Philadelphia, with their shipyards and industrial firms.

Canal boats crossed the river from Lackawaxen, Pennsylvania, to Minisink Ford, New York, at a slackwater dam and rope ferry. But they often ran into rafts of timber being moved downriver, creating many problems. Accounts from the time tell of collisions, fistfights, and lawsuits.

In 1847, the canal's directors brought in John Augustus Roebling to build an aqueduct that would carry the canal over the river. They looked to Roebling because he had built two suspension bridges in western Pennsylvania. His design needed fewer bridge piers, meaning there would be fewer obstructions in the river to block the way of the timber rafts.

The $41,750 aqueduct was ready for the canal's 1848 season and

The Delaware Aqueduct was built in hopes of resolving conflicts between the lumbering and coal mining industries, whose use of the Delaware River to transport their products often led to clashes. The aqueduct was designed by John Roebling, who later built the Brooklyn Bridge.

helped reduce canal travel time by one full day, saving shippers thousands of dollars each year. It was used until 1898, when the canal closed. The aqueduct was later turned into a highway toll bridge and is now honored as the oldest suspension bridge in the country and a forerunner of the Brooklyn Bridge that Roebling started in 1867 and his son completed in 1883.

The two suspension cables are made of wrought iron strands, spun on-site under Roebling's direction. Each 8-1/2-inch diameter suspension cable carries 2,150 wires bunched into seven strands. Laboratory tests in 1983 found that the cable was still viable and some of the wires even exceeded Roebling's specifications. The cable strands are held in place by wrapping wire, which was replaced in 1985, after almost 140 years of use.

The wooden superstructure, made of white pine, was replaced every 25 years by the canal company. The last surviving canal-era timbers were removed in the 1930s. In 1986 the superstructure was reconstructed under National Park Service direction using Roebling's original plans, drawings, notes, and specifications.

VISITORS INFORMATION: The bridge crosses the Delaware River in Lackawaxen. Telephone: (570) 685-4871.
www.nps.gov/upde

ZANE GREY MUSEUM

I've never had any interest in reading novels about the American west. I'd heard of Zane Grey, but didn't know anything about him. I don't know if I'll ever like the western novel, but I certainly have a new appreciation for Grey as a result of visiting the National Park Services' Zane Grey Museum on the banks of the upper Delaware River in Lackawaxen.

The museum is located in a house that Grey lived in after he left a dental practice in New York City and moved to Lackawaxen in hopes of succeeding as a writer. Three rooms in the house hold Zane Grey memorabilia that paints a much broader picture of him than one has by simply associating him with his novels. For instance, he was a world-class sport fisherman and held many records for the largest fish of different species that he caught. Knowledgeable Park Service staff and volunteers conduct tours of the museum, helping visitors to learn about Grey's career and life.

Born Pearl Zane Gray in the family town of Zanesville, Ohio, in 1872, his main interests as a youth were baseball, fishing, and writing. It is reported that he wrote his first book at age 9, and that his father, a farmer, preacher, and dentist, burned it. The elder Gray wanted his son to follow in his footsteps as a dentist, and that's what Zane studied at the University of Pennsylvania, while there on a baseball scholarship. He barely made it through Penn and then moved to New York City to establish a dental practice. Weekends often were spent with his brother in Lackawaxen, canoeing and fishing on the Delaware River.

Encouraged by an editor to write a fishing story that was published in 1902, Grey decided to become a writer. (By this time he had changed the spelling of his last name and dropped his first name, to become Zane Grey.) Following the advice given to writers to write about things you know about, Grey's first book detailed the adventures of a family member, Betty Zane. Publishers refused it, however.

In 1905, Grey married a woman he had met years before at Lackawaxen, Lina Roth, whom he called Dolly. He continued to try to write, but without much commercial success. Then one night in New York City he met Colonel J.C. "Buffalo" Jones, who was organizing an expedition to the west to trap mountain lions. Grey thought that participating in a big adventure might give him the creative spark

Although he lived along the Upper Delaware River, Zane Grey was the leading writer about the American West. He also was an avid outdoorsman who held many sport fishing records and owned a large fleet of boats.

he needed and his wife demonstrated her faith in his ability by giving the last of her inheritance to allow him to buy into the trip. It was a trip that changed his life and ultimately made him the country's richest writer. His account of that trip was published in 1908 as *The Last of the Plainsmen*.

In 1910, Harper and Brothers published *The Heritage of the Desert*, Grey's first western novel and his first real success. That was followed in 1912 by *Riders of the Purple Sage*, the work for which he is best known. By 1915, Grey had 15 books in print (frontier, baseball, juvenile adventure, western) along with fishing and outdoor articles and serialized stories.

Grey's financial success came not as much from his ability, however, as from Dolly's abilities. She edited all of his stories and books and also negotiated all of his contracts. While he would have accepted just enough money for a book to finance his next trip, she negotiated much larger payments. And while he didn't care at all about his stories being made into movies, she negotiated seven-year movie contracts and then sold the rights to the same story again after the seven years had passed. The earnings went to finance Grey's passions; at one time, he had 50 boats in the fleet he owned. He was so wealthy even during the Depression that he spent more than $250,000 on a boat during those economically distressed times.

Unfortunately, Grey's appreciation for his wife's abilities did not extend to treating her with respect. She stayed home with their three children while he traveled, often in the company of a secretary. He spent most of his spare time fishing and at one time or another held all of the deep-sea fishing records, including two that remain unbroken today.

In 1937, while fishing with his son Romer on Oregon's Rogue River, he suffered a stroke. He recuperated at his home in Altadena, Calif., and was able to make one more fishing expedition, this time to Australia. On October 23, 1939, after completing his morning exercise workout at his Altadena home, he had a heart attack and died. After Dolly's death in 1957, the ashes of the two of them were interred in the Lutheran Church cemetery down the street from what is now the museum.

VISITORS INFORMATION: The museum is located along the banks of the Delaware River on Scenic Drive.
Telephone: (570) 685-4871.

Left: Writer Zane Grey studied to be a dentist at the University of Pennsylvania but never really wanted to practice his profession and was happy to abandon it in favor of having wilderness adventures and writing about them. **Above:** The Little Mud Pond Swamp at **SHOHOLA FALLS** is part of the Shohola Recreation Area, between Milford and Hawley, that includes 1,150 acres of state game lands located within state forest land. The falls plunge over a series of drops on their way into a rocky gorge. There is a path from which one can see over the falls in various locations.

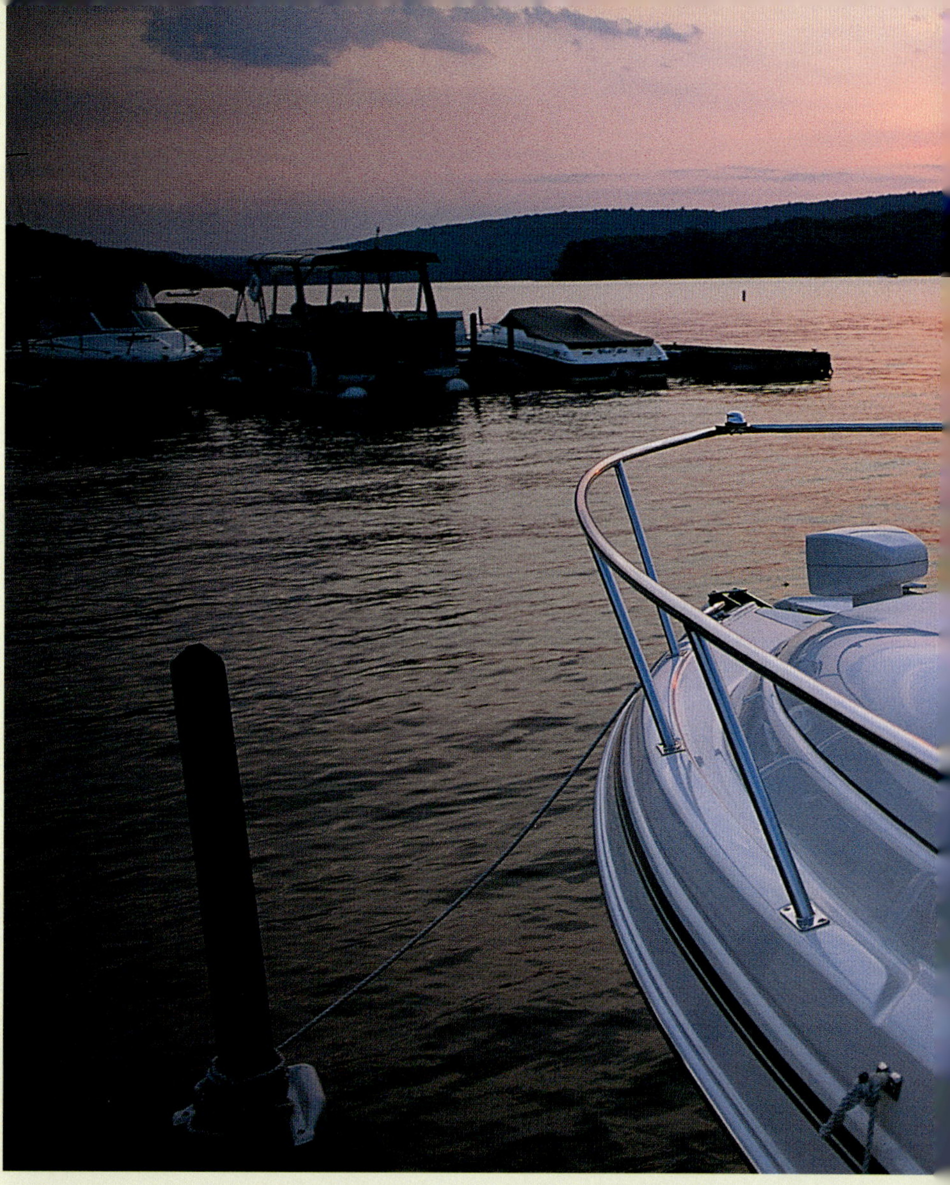

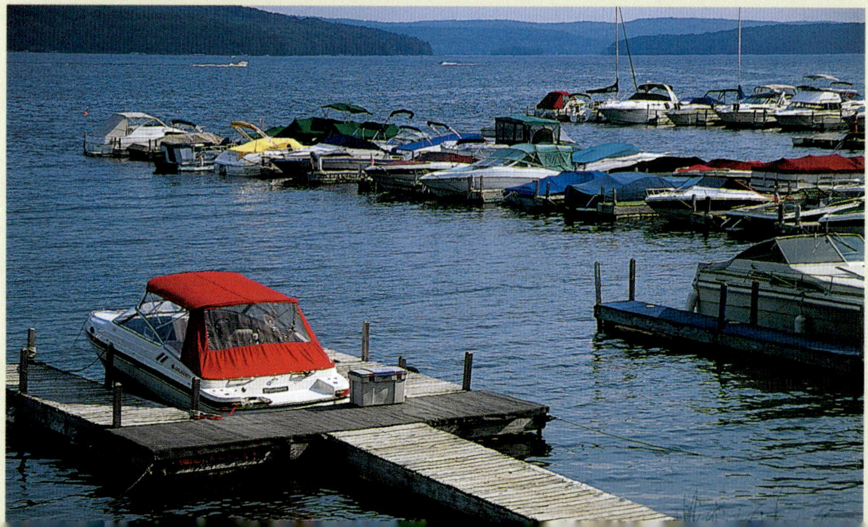

Above: There are many places at which one can see beautiful sunsets along U.S. Route 6, including here over **LAKE WALLENPAUPACK**. **Left:** Built in 1927 by Pennsylvania Power and Light Company, **LAKE WALLENPAUPACK** has 52 miles of shoreline around its 5,700 acres. There are six recreation areas around the lake with hiking trails, campsites, and boat docking slips. Also around the lake are many lakefront and lakeview homes. The original survey of the lake region shows that there was a 12,150-acre parcel of land that was transferred from the William Penn estate to James Wilson, who was one of only four men who signed both the Declaration of Independence in 1776 and the Constitution of the United States in 1787.

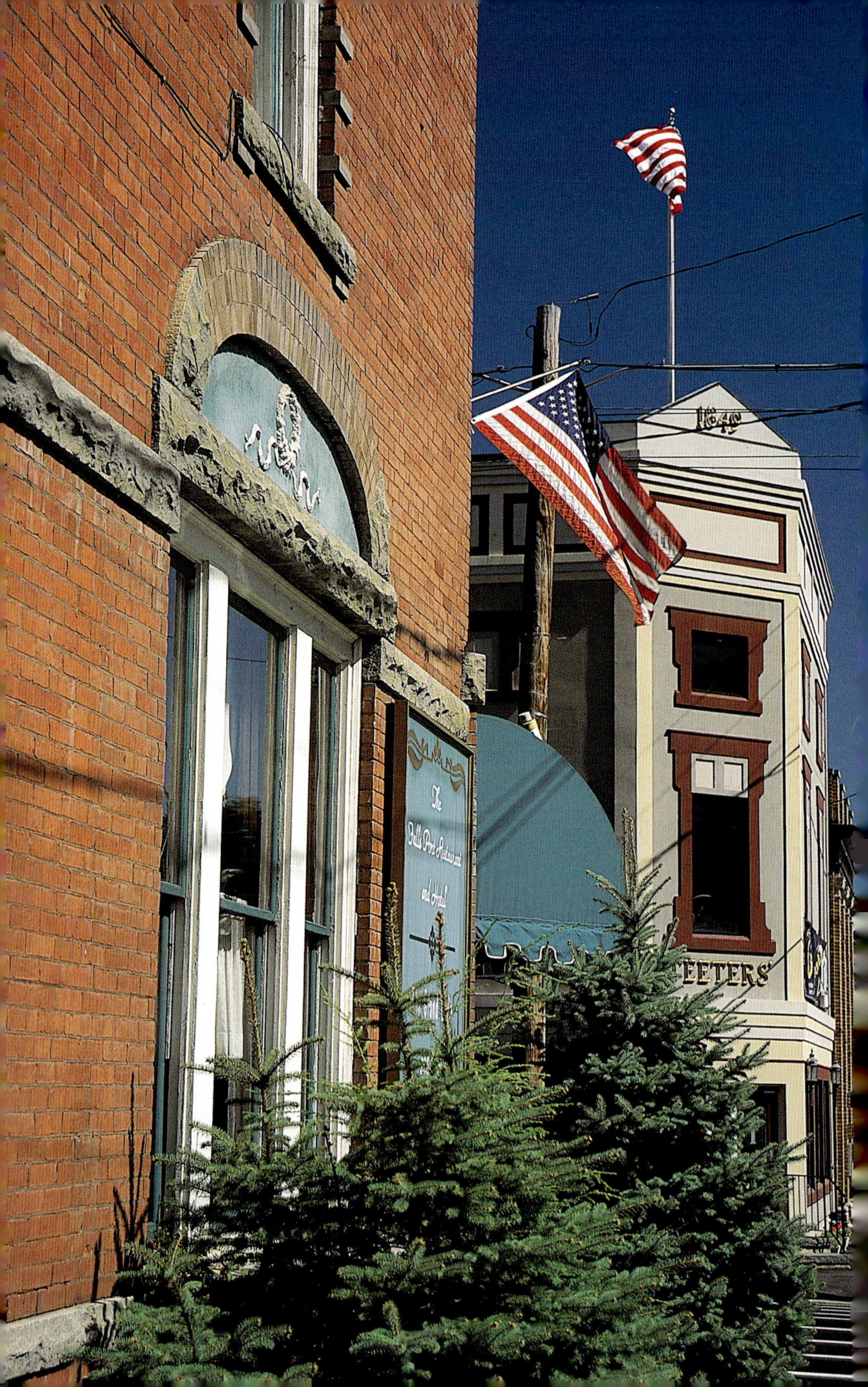

Left: The historic **FALLS PORT INN IN HAWLEY** is a restored Victorian inn whose guest rooms and dining rooms are filled with antiques and elegant décor. At first the town was known as Paupack Eddy. It was renamed Falls Port, then Hawleysburgh, in honor of Irad Hawley, the first president of the Pennsylvania Coal Company. Finally in 1851, the name was shortened to its present name, Hawley. **Below:** Visitors to the Pocono Mountains can enjoy the cheerful comfort of the **SETTLERS INN AT BINGHAM PARK, HAWLEY.** There are 20 overnight rooms and suites decorated with quilted bed covers, wicker, and antiques. The idea of building a community hotel started in the 1920s when the hydroelectric dam was being constructed nearby. Community leaders went door-to-door selling shares in the hotel. A local architect designed the building at no charge and construction began in 1927 on land that had been in the old Delaware and Hudson canal bed. But the Depression and other events conspired against the project, and it wasn't until the building was bought by its present owners in 1980 that it was returned to its original use.

Dorflinger Glass Museum
Dorflinger-Suydam Wildlife Sanctuary

At age 18, Christian Dorflinger, who was born in the Alsace-Lorraine region of France and learned the art of glassmaking as an apprentice to his uncle, came to the United States in 1846 and worked in a glass factory in Camden, N.J. Six years later he opened his own factory in Brooklyn, New York, making kerosene lamp chimneys. Within 10 years he had opened two more glass factories, including the Greenpoint Flint Glass Works.

In the 1860s, Dorflinger purchased 600 acres of land in northeastern Pennsylvania to be used as an escape from the stresses of his work in the factories. Shortly after relocating, he built a factory in White Mills, and during his time there designed and produced some of the finest lead crystal in the country. The company operated in White Mills until 1921, six years after Christian Dorflinger's death.

The Dorflinger Glass Museum opened about 10 years ago so visitors could see and appreciate Dorflinger's extraordinary craftsmanship and use of color. There is a self-guiding tour of the several display cases that helps explain the various pieces that are displayed. Try to come on a sunny day; the sun streaming through the windows and onto the colored glass is absolutely magnificent. This definitive collection of Dorflinger's art ranges from household items to presentation pieces, from the graceful elegance of simplicity to the unbelievably complex.

Dorflinger's grandson, Fred Suydam, acquired the property in the early 1920s and used it as a second home with his wife, caring for it for more than 50 years. Their donation of the home to the community has allowed everyone to enjoy the natural beauty of the trails and plantings.

VISITORS INFORMATION: The Wildlife Sanctuary and Glass Museum are on Elizabeth Street, up a steep hill from U.S. Route 6 in White Mills, between Hawley and Honesdale. Telephone: (570) 253-1185.   www.dorflinger.com

Left: Beautiful examples of Christian Dorflinger's artistry and skill at glassmaking are on display at the Dorflinger Glass Museum. **Below:** The grounds surrounding the Dorflinger Glass Museum have walking trails and a lake, perfect for nature study and a summer arts and music festival.

Above: **HONESDALE**, Wayne County seat, was founded in 1826 by the Delaware and Hudson Canal Co. and Jason Torrey, a pioneer settler. Its original name was "Dyberry Forks." Washington Irving, author of Rip Van Winkle and many other noted stories, visited the area early-on with his friend, Philip Hone, who was president of the Delaware & Hudson Canal Company, and one of the first mayors of New York City. Irving called the town "Honesdale" in honor of his friend; Hone, in return, named a perpendicular ledge of rocks that overlooks the center of town "Irving," for his friend. **Top Right: HONESDALE** is where the first commercial steam locomotive was used in the United States. Imported from England, the Stourbridge Lion made its initial run on August 8, 1829, but had to be withdrawn from service because it was too heavy for the rails. Today the local Chamber of Commerce operates rail excursions through the prime tourist season.

Bottom Right: In addition to many beautiful inns that provide overnight lodging for travelers, visitors along U.S. Route 6 also have many opportunities to enjoy fine food. The **ALPINE INN IN HONESDALE** is a good example of the wide variety of unique eateries that range from diners to beautiful dining rooms.

37

LACKAWANNA COUNTY

Below: **CARBONDALE** is the fourth oldest city in the state, older than its larger neighbors Scranton and Wilkes-Barre. Seen here from the Carbondale Plaza are St. Rose of Lima Church and monuments to Christopher Columbus and veterans of the Civil War, Spanish-American War, and World Wars I and II.

Left: The **LACKAWANNA COUNTY COURTHOUSE** in Scranton was built on land donated by the Lackawanna Iron and Coal Company that was owned by the Scranton family. Before the courthouse could be built from 1881 to 1884, the land had to be drained and filled with dirt and slag from the family's iron furnaces. Built in West Mountain sandstone, the courthouse's architecture is a mix of Victorian Gothic and Romanesque.

Electric City Trolley Station and Museum

When I was growing up in inner-city Philadelphia, one of the things we would do on weekends was to go to the suburbs to ride either the Philadelphia & Western or Red Arrow trolley lines out to a neighboring community. Our family didn't have a car and so all of our travel was by public transportation. As odd as it may sound now, it actually was a lot of fun to see the nice homes and green spaces outside the city. We'd ride the trolleys to the end of the line, get off and get some ice cream at a store nearby, and then ride back into the city again.

All of this is to say that I have fond memories of old trolleys and thus was thrilled to run across Red Arrow and P&W cars in the collection at the Electric City museum, housed in a restored late 19th century mill building just across the parking lot from Steamtown in Scranton. (For someone like me, a railroading site and a trolley site in the same location was almost too much to take in one day.)

The Electric City Trolley Museum in Scranton was developed by the Lackawanna Heritage Valley Authority and is managed by Lackawanna County adjacent to Steamtown National Historic Site.

Rather than take Steamtown's rail excursion, I opted for a trolley ride on a 1926 Red Arrow car that goes out to the historic Scranton iron furnaces. The 48-foot-long car weighs 29.5 tons and has a crew of two, a motorman and a conductor. Boarding is through the center doors and most of its 62 seats can be moved to face front or back. Operating controls are at both ends of the car because there weren't turntables on the lines, meaning the car would go out of Philadelphia to Media, Sharon Hill, or some other community and then head back into the city with the operator moving from one end to the other.

The car in the Electric City collection is authentic, with old advertising cards lining the ceiling. There's the Lone Ranger promoting Bond Bread (which used to be delivered to our front door by a route man, along with my favorite chocolate donuts), and a promotion for Campbell's vegetable soups that can be eaten on "Lent, Fridays, any day."

Future plans call for the trolley rides to be extended to the Laurel

Line tunnel and a visitors center to be built at Montage, outside of Scranton.

After my ride, I went through the museum, which has several cars as well as exhibits and video displays that pay tribute to the way in which trolleys linked communities and also helped develop recreational opportunities by taking city dwellers to rural picnic grounds often owned by the trolley companies.

VISITORS INFORMATION: The Electric City Trolley Station and Museum shares an entrance with Steamtown National Historic Site at Lackawanna and Cliff Avenues, Scranton. Telephone: (570) 963-6590.

In 1887, Scranton was Pennsylvania's first city to have a fully-electrified trolley line and became known as "The Electric City."

Steamtown National Historic Site in Scranton pays loving tribute to the golden age of steam engines in our nation's transportation history.

Steamtown National Historic Site

There's something about the sight of a mammoth locomotive and the sound of steam hissing underneath a haunting train whistle that gets my heart racing and adrenaline flowing. So Steamtown is my kind of place.

Operated as a historic site by the National Park Service, Steamtown pays tribute to a part of American railroading that hasn't existed for nearly 50 years—the era of the steam locomotive. The site is on 40 acres

43

of the Scranton rail yard that was operated by the Delaware, Lackawanna, and Western Railroad (DL&W), one of the earliest rail lines in this part of the commonwealth.

The Steamtown collection of rolling stock includes locomotives, freight cars, passenger cars, and maintenance-of-way equipment from several historic railroads. The locomotives range in size from a "tiny" industrial switcher engine to a huge Union Pacific Big Boy built in 1941. The oldest engine there is a 1903 freight engine built for the Chicago Union Transfer Railway Company.

We start in the Visitors Center with its interactive TV-based displays and quizzes that help us understand the various elements of railroading on the DL&W. When we go into the theatre, we're greeted by the sound of a train chugging along, its whistle blaring, as we find our seats and prepare to watch an 18-minute movie. "Steel and Steam" is the story of a young boy who grows up with the DL&W and then works for it when he is grown.

Find out when the ranger programs will be held and plan to attend those that are of particular interest to you. The rangers are knowledgeable and bring the era to life through their presentations.

We leave the visitor center and move on to the history museum, with exhibits that highlight the people and history of steam railroading. Displays cover early railroads, life on the railroad, and the relationship between the railroads and labor, business, and government.

A portion of a roundhouse that was in the Scranton yards from 1902 to 1937 has been rehabilitated and now stores, maintains, and displays engines from the Steamtown collection. Keep your eye peeled outside and if you see an engine starting to move, go out to see how the 90-foot diameter turntable maneuvers engines toward the roundhouse.

The technology museum shows the technological changes and

Visitors to the National Park Service's Steamtown National Historic Site can learn how a steam engine moves heavy trains down the tracks in this exhibit.

advances in railroading through the years, with exhibits on steam locomotive design, railroad architecture, track design and engineering, signals, communications, and railroad safety.

On certain days, there are two-hour, 26-mile rail excursions between Steamtown and Moscow, Pa., over the former DL&W mainline. Other days there are short interpretive steam or diesel train rides within the park's boundaries.

Although railroading's heyday has long passed, it's important that Steamtown and other places like it are keeping alive such an important part of our nation's industrial heritage for future generations to see and learn from. And there's always that sound of rushing steam and haunting whistle to give people like me a thrill.

VISITORS INFORMATION: Steamtown National Historic Site is at the intersection of Lackawanna and Cliff Avenues in downtown Scranton. Telephone: (570) 340-5200.
www.nps.gov/stea

Pennsylvania Anthracite Heritage Museum

Located in Scranton's McDade Park, the Pennsylvania Anthracite Heritage Museum, operated by the Pennsylvania Historical and Museum Commission, tells the story of life and work in the northeastern corner of Pennsylvania when hard anthracite coal powered the country's industrial revolution. The museum is located next to the Lackawanna Coal Mine, which takes visitors underground for a hands-on experience of what it was like to be a miner.

An orientation video at the museum tells of the immigrants who came to northeastern Pennsylvania looking for work and ended up mining anthracite, which is nearly pure carbon and burns very hot with little smoke and ash.

Exhibits throughout the museum emphasize the point that hard work was the key to survival and success of the immigrants in their new home. It must have been very scary for them to leave everything they knew and come across the ocean to a new land. One thing that made it easier was the tendency of people to settle in neighborhoods together with the churches and other groups that helped them preserve their culture and heritage.

Working the coal mines was a family activity. Children as young as six years old were in the breakers, picking slate from the coal. While the men and older boys worked in the mines, the women and girls worked outside, cooking, cleaning, and preparing baths for the dirty miners. Some families took in boarders to get a bit more income. Those men were given a place to sleep, meals, and bathing privileges.

In the late 19th century, many of the women and girls worked in silk and lace factories that were built throughout the area. In 1910, there were 20,000 women and 5,000 girls employed in those factories.

The museum is short on modern interactive exhibits, but has interesting displays with explanatory text that cover the work ethic of the immigrants, coal mining techniques, medicine and health care of the time, heritage and culture of the families, and the silk mills.

Mining and milling machinery is shown, as is an example of a "corner tap," the barroom the men would go to after work to talk about the union and efforts to better their conditions.

There are galleries on home life and the church, but not on education, because children were expected to work to help support the family rather than go to school.

VISITORS INFORMATION: The museum is in Scranton's McDade Park. Telephone: (570) 963-4804.
www.visitnepa.org

Previous Page: Anthracite mining was a way of life for all members of the family. Displayed at the Anthracite Heritage Museum are these shoes worn by Evan Jenkins when he was a "breaker boy," working at the coal breaker before he was old enough to go down in the mines. **Below:** For many years, anthracite coal mining was the economic lifeblood of northeastern Pennsylvania. Items used in the mines are displayed at the Pennsylvania Historical and Museum Commission's Anthracite Heritage Museum in Scranton.

Lackawanna Coal Mine

While the Pennsylvania Anthracite Heritage Museum tells a lot about the life of coal miners in the anthracite mines, it's not the same as actually going down in a mine yourself to see and feel what it was like. Visitors can go 300 feet below ground at the Lackawanna Coal Mine, next to the Anthracite Heritage Museum in Scranton's McDade Park.

Although it was warm on the surface the day I toured the mine, it was naturally air conditioned and cool below ground. Accompanied by a former miner, we entered a mine car, being careful not to hit our heads on the low roof, and set off down a steep incline, so steep that it became difficult to sit upright in the car.

During the tour we developed an appreciation for the difficult life of the men and boys who worked the mines. It must have been very hard to spend hours in cramped, cold, and damp circumstances, always having the fear of a deadly explosion in the back of your mind.

We learned how coal was blasted from veins in the walls, how pillars were left to support the underground rooms, and how mule-drawn carts took the coal to the surface. We learned about the ways the miners checked for dangerous methane gas and the reliance they placed on their candles and battery-powered lamps. At one point, our guide turned out the electric lights so we could see how utterly dark and black it was in the mine without any light source. Those of us on the tour couldn't see our own hands in front of our faces, much less anyone else standing next to us.

As we left the mine, we each were given a certificate attesting to the fact that we had "satisfactorily completed the course of instruction by a competent mine foreman and found to be duly qualified to be employed as an anthracite miner in the Slope 190 Mine, Scranton, Pa." I appreciate the honor, but I don't think that's how I want to spend my time, if I can help it. It's hard to imagine what the miners went through, and the tour fills you with admiration for the people who helped our country grow in this way.

VISITORS INFORMATION: The Lackawanna Coal Mine is in McDade Park, Scranton. Telephone: (570) 963-MINE or (800) 238-7245. www.visitnepa.org

Visitors to Scranton can experience what it is like to mine anthracite coal 300 feet beneath the ground on the Lackawanna County Mine Tour in Scranton's McDade Park, across from the Anthracite Heritage Museum.

LACKAWANNA STATION, Scranton, was built in 1908 as a passenger station and the administrative headquarters of the Delaware, Lackawanna, and Western Railroad. When the line merged with the Erie Railroad, the combined headquarters was moved to the western part of the state, diminishing the role of this grand station complex. Fortunately, commercial interests restored the building and converted it to use as a hotel. The crowning achievement was the revitalization of the grand lobby, which incorporated a dramatically ornamented mosaic tile floor, barrel vaulted Tiffany stained-glass ceiling, rare Sienna marble walls, and the unique faience tile murals that surround it.

SCRANTON'S EVERHART MUSEUM OF NATURAL HISTORY, SCIENCE AND ART was founded by Dr. Isaiah Fawkes Everhart in 1908. A physician and businessman, Dr. Everhart held a fond interest in natural history. After serving in the Civil War, he decided to assemble a comprehensive collection of Pennsylvania's native birds and animals. A skilled taxidermist, he started a collection of mounted specimens that expanded into one of the finest and largest collections in the United States. Although the museum's focus initially was on natural history, it added fine arts and other collections over the years, making it a "museum for everyone." Shown in the foreground of this gallery photo is a painting by American artist John Frederick Kensett.

Above: Not all the antiques along U.S. Route 6 are found in charming inns. There are many antique shops like **Carriage House Antiques in Clarks Summit** to delight travelers searching for that perfect piece for their home.

Right: Mountains and rivers are the key geographic elements across the northern tier of Pennsylvania. The **Susquehanna River**, the nation's 16th largest river, originates in New York State and flows south through Pennsylvania and into Maryland, emptying in the Atlantic Ocean.

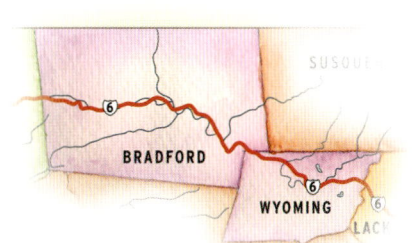

Endless Mountains

Tunkhannock Viaduct

As you drive north from U.S. Route 6 towards the small town of Nicholson ("Population 1,000, Hospitality A MILLION"), the Tunkhannock Viaduct suddenly looms before you, a mammoth structure obviously out of place in this little village.

In the early 1900s, the board of directors of the Delaware, Lackawanna & Western Railroad decided that their line's track bed was too hilly, and undertook a major reconstruction project. The biggest challenge was finding a better way across the Tunkhannock Creek valley. To eliminate a difficult, steep climb, a viaduct had to be constructed nearly one-half mile long, more than 200 feet above the valley floor.

At that time, no modern bridge of that scale ever had been built. Architect A. Burton Cohen took his inspiration from the ancient aqueduct at Pont du Gard, Rome, with its tiers of arches.

Rather than use cut stone as the Romans did, those who built the viaduct over Nicholson turned to steel-reinforced concrete. Tall towers were constructed at both ends of the proposed bridge and cables were strung between them. Large buckets of cement were sent out the cables and poured into wooden forms that were built around the steel reinforcing rods. The viaduct required 10 spans of 180 feet to cross the valley floor. On each arched span are 11 smaller arches that provide light, honeycomb-like strength to support the railbed that runs across the top.

Construction took three years and used more than two million pounds of reinforcing steel and more than 163,000 cubic yards of concrete. Freight trains still use the bridge today, along with tourist trains from the Steamtown National Historic Site in Scranton.

Visitors Information: The viaduct is in Nicholson on Pa. Route 92 north of U.S. Route 6.

Before the Tunkhannock Viaduct was built at Nicholson, it took five engines to haul freight trains between Clarks Summit and Hallstead. It took three years to build the 2,375-foot-long bridge, which has been referred to as "the height wonder of the world" and "the eighth wonder of the world."

TUNKHANNOCK, gateway to the Endless Mountains, is the county seat of Wyoming County. This sidewalk mural reminds visitors of the friendly reception they receive in the Endless Mountains and throughout the northern tier.

Wyalusing is at the confluence of the Susquehanna River and Wyalusing Creek in southeast Bradford County. The Iroquois Indians used the nearby Wyalusing Rocks as a signaling point. A Moravian mission was established in the area in 1765 to bring Christianity to the Delaware Indians. The town's Main Street has many restored 19th century buildings including the 1894 Wyalusing Hotel and the 1860 Miller's Pharmacy.

The **WYALUSING ROCKS OVERLOOK** along U.S. Route 6 a mile west of town is a particularly good place to stop to see the types of land that make up the area. The site was a sacred area for the Indians native to the region. Here visitors can see the rich farmland of nearby Terry Township.

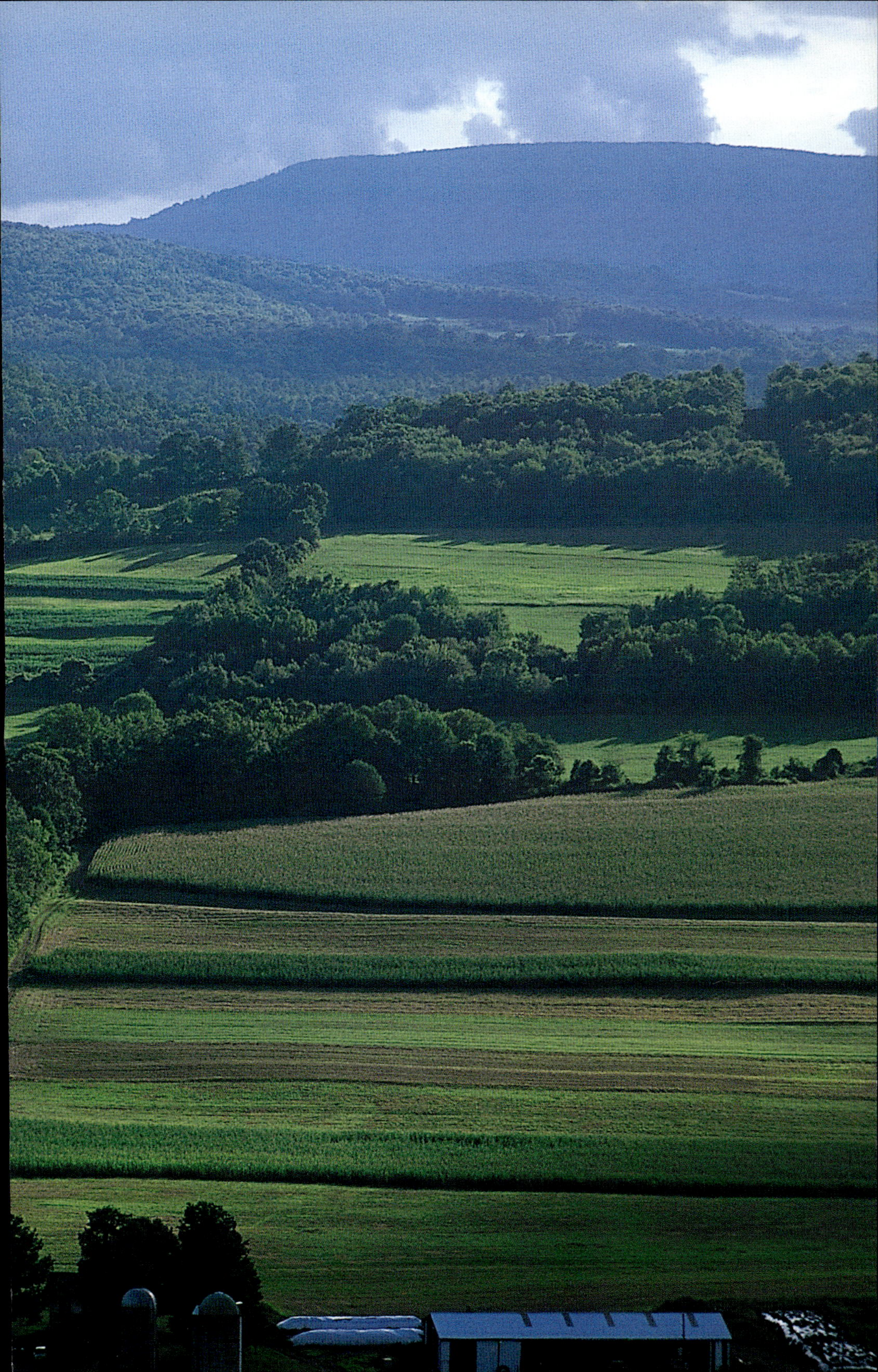

WYALUSING OVERLOOK

Although the scenery along much of U.S. 6 can be very attractive, and convince the unsure just how much of Pennsylvania still is forested, a scenic overlook outside Wyalusing is particularly nice because of a display there on landscape conservation measures that can be seen from the overlook — contour stripcropping,

The Wyalusing Rocks Overlook also provides a particularly good view of the Susquehanna River. A railroad that follows the course of the river was built on the towpath of the North Branch Canal.

diversions, manure storage system, barnyard runoff control, streamside buffers, bank stabilization, land use, and the Susquehanna River.

As you motor along, take a few minutes to pull off at the Wyalusing Overlook and learn something about the land you are going by; it's well worth it.

VISITORS INFORMATION: The overlook is on the south side of U.S. 6, west of Wyalusing.

French Azilum

Even though none of the original buildings remain, a tour of French Azilum near Towanda gives visitors a sense of the settlement along the Susquehanna River that was built for refugees fleeing the French Revolution.

In the late 18th century, three Americans who were sympathetic to the plight of refugees who were loyal to the king of France, or who had fled mulatto and slave uprisings in Santo Domingo (now Haiti), saw an opportunity to help the refugees and also to make some money for themselves. Robert Morris, John Nicholson, and Stephen Girard formed a land company and bought 1,600 acres on which to establish Azilum.

In the LaPorte house that was the home of U.S. Congressman John LaPorte, who was born at Azilum in 1798, one can see a map that shows the large community that was planned. The group used 300 acres for a planned town with a two-acre market square, a gridiron pattern of broad streets, and 413 housing lots. Farm areas for the houses were located away from the town, with each house having its own farm plot. Initially in 1794, 30 rough log houses were built. There also were stores, a brewery, and other buildings.

Although the living quarters were rough and crude, many had chimneys, wallpaper, window glass, shutters, and porches to satisfy the desire of those who lived in them for beauty and comfort. The residents also had some of the luxuries and extravagances brought from their native lands to help them remember those better days.

The most impressive building was the two-story log structure known as "La Grande Maison." At 84 feet long and 60 feet wide, it had numerous small-paned windows and eight large fireplaces. There are unconfirmed reports that it was to be the dwelling of Marie Antoinette, queen of France, had she come to Azilum with her two children.

Unfortunately, the settlement did not last longer than 10 years, victim to economic factors, including the bankruptcy of Morris and Nicholson, and a changing political climate that made it possible for the émigrés to return to Santo Domingo or France.

Only a few families, including the LaPortes, stayed in the area and helped settle nearby communities.

French Azilum (Asylum) was a planned community built to house French exiles who remained loyal to their king during the French Revolution. It was occupied from 1793 to 1803. None of the original buildings erected by the exiles remains today, although some foundations have been uncovered at an archaeological dig on the site.

The LaPorte House, built in 1836 by the son of one of the original settlers of French Azilum, is open to the public.

The historic site today covers more than 20 acres of the original settlement. It is managed by a non-profit group and administered by the Pennsylvania Historical and Museum Commission. Visitors enter through a small wooden building to obtain tickets and purchase historic documents relating to Azilum and other souvenirs. Guided tours of the LaPorte house are included in the admission price, along with a self-guided tour of the grounds.

Most people start in the museum cabin, which has a video that tells the story of French Azilum. A sign on the VCR indicates the video can be temperamental, and that was the case the day I was there, so I was unable to view it. Also in the cabin are exhibits on the history of the families that lived at Azilum. You'll see items like a candlestick used by the French, lace pieces worn by women in the 18th century, a copper bed warmer, and things found during a 1956 excavation. On the wall is a portrait of Marie Antoinette.

Also on the grounds tour are cabins with exhibits on maple sugaring, tools of the era, and spinning, weaving, and dyeing. There is a gazebo, an herb garden, and a bell from a nearby ferry that operated from the early 1800s until the 1930s. The wine-root cellar was excavated in 1956-57 and several artifacts were found, including bottles, glassware, and ironware.

The day I visited was the last day that a summer archeological dig from Binghamton College in New York was working on the grounds. In their three years, they had uncovered the foundation of a building from 1790. From historic records, the students and professors knew the building contained a living room, dining room, and kitchen, and they still were unsure which portion they had uncovered. They told me that in addition to the stone foundation, they had found some nails and rodent bones.

Down the hill, little flags in the ground indicated where sensitive instruments had determined that other sites might be located, and it is expected that other digs will be held there in future years.

After I talked with the folks at the dig, I made my way to the LaPorte house for the guided tour that occurs every hour. There is an interesting combination of original and other furniture and furnishings inside. Ceilings were stenciled by an itinerant painter and a fireplace screen with a peacock motif was originally purchased in France and owned by James Buchanan, the only U.S. president from Pennsylvania.

A melodion in one of the rooms (a combination piano and organ) has the likeness of famed singer Jenny Lind carved into each of its four legs. The house also contains an original dropleaf dining table and dinnerware, a Royal Doulton bowl, and a "mammy rocker" — a settee-length bench with a railing along part of it that would keep a baby on the bench while the mother sat at the end and rocked it back and forth.

VISITORS INFORMATION: To reach French Azilum, go 4 miles south of Towanda on Pa. Rte. 187 and then four miles east on SR 2014, following directional signs. Telephone: (570) 265-3376. www.frenchazilum.org

Above: The **BRADFORD COUNTY COURTHOUSE AND HISTORICAL MUSEUM** is one of the main attractions in Towanda. **Top Right:** The **BRADFORD COUNTY REGIONAL ARTS COUNCIL** has restored and is operating historic theatres in Towanda, Sayre, and Canton. Towanda's Keystone Theatre started life in 1886 as Hale's Opera House. The facility deteriorated as live stage shows gave way to movies and audiences grew smaller while operating costs increased. The council took on the project in 1988 and undertook a number of restoration activities through1996. **Bottom Right:** This Victorian Bed and Breakfast in the York Avenue community of **TOWANDA** is one of many unique B&B's along U.S. Route 6.

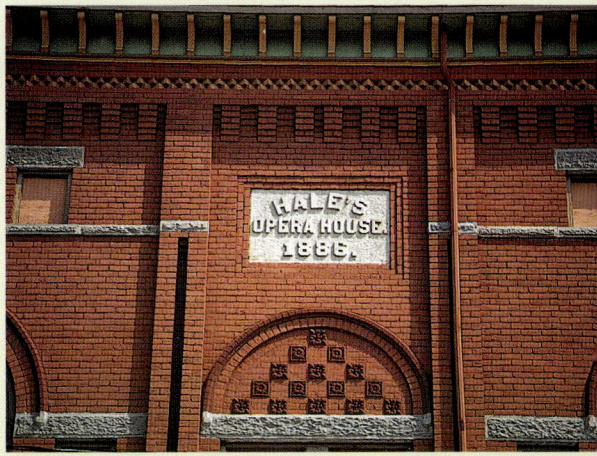

Above Left: This 100-foot-long covered bridge is of Theodore Burr Arch Truss design. It was built in 1853, although the name of the builder has disappeared in history. The bridge spans **SUGAR CREEK** on township route 554 off U.S. Route 6 northeast of Luther Mills. **Above Right:** This 19th century Methodist Episcopal church is on the National Register of Historic Sites. It is located one mile west of **BURLINGTON**. The graveyard associated with the church has tombstones dating back to 1808. **Right:** Midway between Troy and Towanda, **MT. PISGAH STATE PARK** is two miles north of U.S. Route 6 along Mill Creek at the base of Mt. Pisgah. A dam on Mill Creek created Stephen Foster Lake in the park, named for the American composer who at one time lived in the area. The land that became Mt. Pisgah State Park was first cleared for farmland in the early 1800s. Many of the early settlers came from New England and their descendants still live in the area. The park's environmental education center is dedicated to the early settlers, and an early family cemetery has been restored and is part of the park's interpretive system.

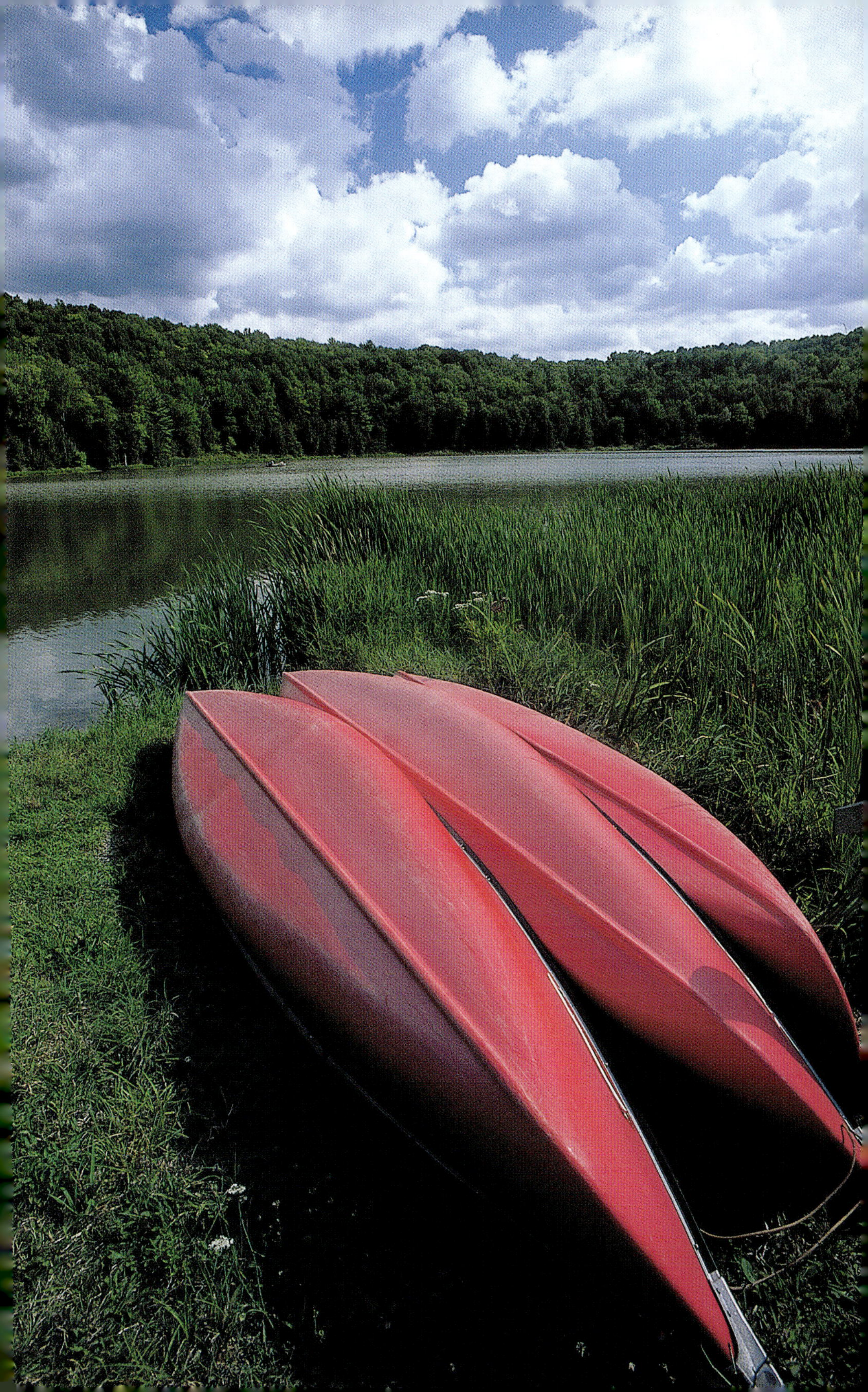

Heading west of **Troy** on U.S. Route 6, travelers once again see beautiful Pennsylvania farmland.

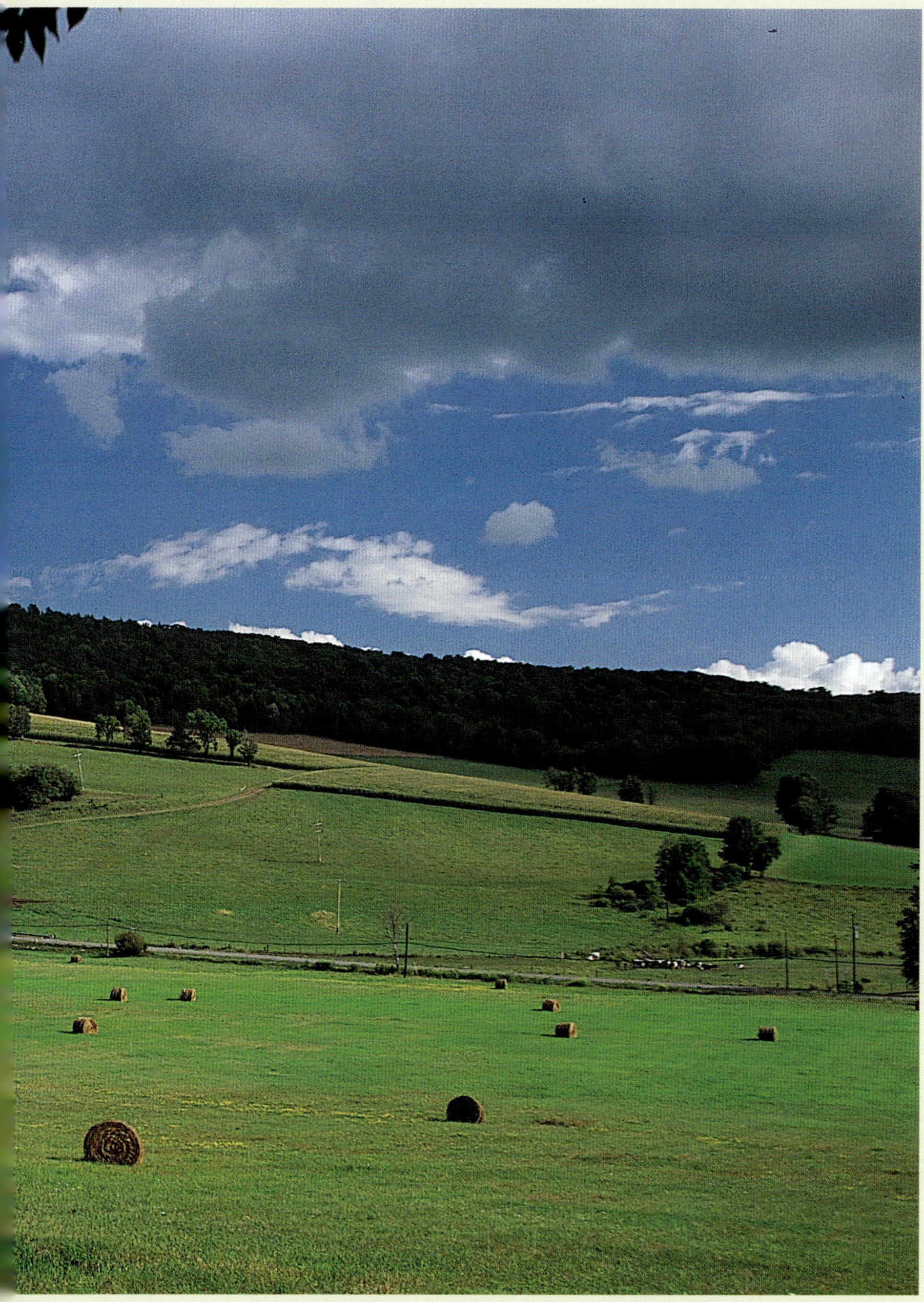

Right: The **VAN DYNE CIVIC BUILDING IN TROY**, Bradford County, has had three distinct lives. Troy once was a co-county seat with Towanda because of the difficulty in traveling to Towanda by horse and buggy from the western part of the county. In 1870, the General Assembly named Troy a "Half-Shire" town and authorized it to host court sessions twice a year. The Troy Half-Shire Courthouse, opened in 1894, is the only one known to exist in the state. In 1917 the building was reborn as the Van Dyne Civic Building, and in 1980 it became the Troy office of Citizens and Northern Bank after a complete exterior restoration and landscaping and interior remodeling. It is a National Historic Landmark and is on the National Register of Historic Places. **Below:** What is now Mansfield University started as **MANSFIELD CLASSICAL SEMINARY**, built and opened in 1857. Within a year it had burned to the ground, leaving 150 students with no place to go. The residents of the town raised funds to rebuild the school and by 1859 it was once again open. In 1862 it became a state normal school and later a state teachers college, and state college, before becoming a university that is part of the Pennsylvania State System of Higher Education.

CITIZENS & NORTHERN BANK

Tioga & Potter Counties

Above: WELLSBORO'S PACKER PARK has a variety of recreational opportunities for residents and visitors. **Left:** The land on which **HILLS CREEK STATE PARK** stands, originally known as Kelly's Swamp, was purchased in 1950. Within this swamp, at the present location of the swimming beach, was a small mine from which pigment for the paint industry was extracted. The park opened in 1953 and is named for the creek that runs through it. The stream was named after Captain William Hill, who settled in the area around 1820. The focal point of the park is a 137-acre lake developed by impounding Hills Creek. The general area now covered by water has almost continually, since the end of the last ice age, been under the influence of beaver dams and beavers. Beavers still abound in the area, including Hills Creek Lake. The beaver marsh (vegetation and sediment) is as much as 20 feet deep.

Grand Canyon of Pennsylvania

Many years ago, when I worked as Director of Public Information for what was then the Pennsylvania Department of Environmental Resources, I went along when the agency's Citizens Advisory Council took a float trip down Pine Creek through the Grand Canyon of Pennsylvania. It was my first view of this natural wonder with its spectacular scenery.

Then, a few years ago, I got up early one morning and drove north from Harrisburg with my mountain bike to ride a portion of the gravel rail trail that goes through the canyon. It again was a spectacular trip, this time made more special because I saw a black bear drinking from the creek not far from where I was pedaling. Area outfitters can help you with bike and float trips through the canyon, and there also are opportunities to ride horseback or in Conestoga Wagons.

And, just as in Arizona, sunrises and sunsets from the overlooks at Pennsylvania's Grand Canyon are not to be missed.

The fact that the canyon, which is 47 miles long and more than 1,000 feet deep, is just a few miles west of the thoroughly delightful Victorian town of Wellsboro only adds to the pleasure one gets from being in the area. The east rim is within Leonard Harrison State Park, while the west rim is in Colton Point State Park. You owe it to yourself to experience the pleasures of each season at the Canyon and in Wellsboro.

There are many fine restaurants of various types in Wellsboro and the surrounding area, but one of our special favorites for coming back from trips to the area is the Turkey Ranch on U.S. 15 about 30 minutes south of Wellsboro.

VISITORS INFORMATION: The Grand Canyon of Pennsylvania is on Pa. Route 660, 10 miles west of Wellsboro. Telephone: (570) 724-3061.
www.dcnr.state.pa.us or www.visittiogapa.com

Left: The 47-mile-long Pine Creek Gorge is commonly called the Grand Canyon of Pennsylvania. It is 1,450 feet at its deepest point. There is a Pennsylvania State Park on each side of the canyon. Visitors can boat Pine Creek through the canyon, ride horses on trails in the area, and bike on Pine Creek Trail, a former railroad right-of-way. **Next Pages:** Leonard Harrison State Park, in the Grand Canyon of Pennsylvania, honors a civic-minded Wellsboro resident who gave 121 acres of picnic ground he owned to the state in 1922. Additional lands were added in the late 1940s.

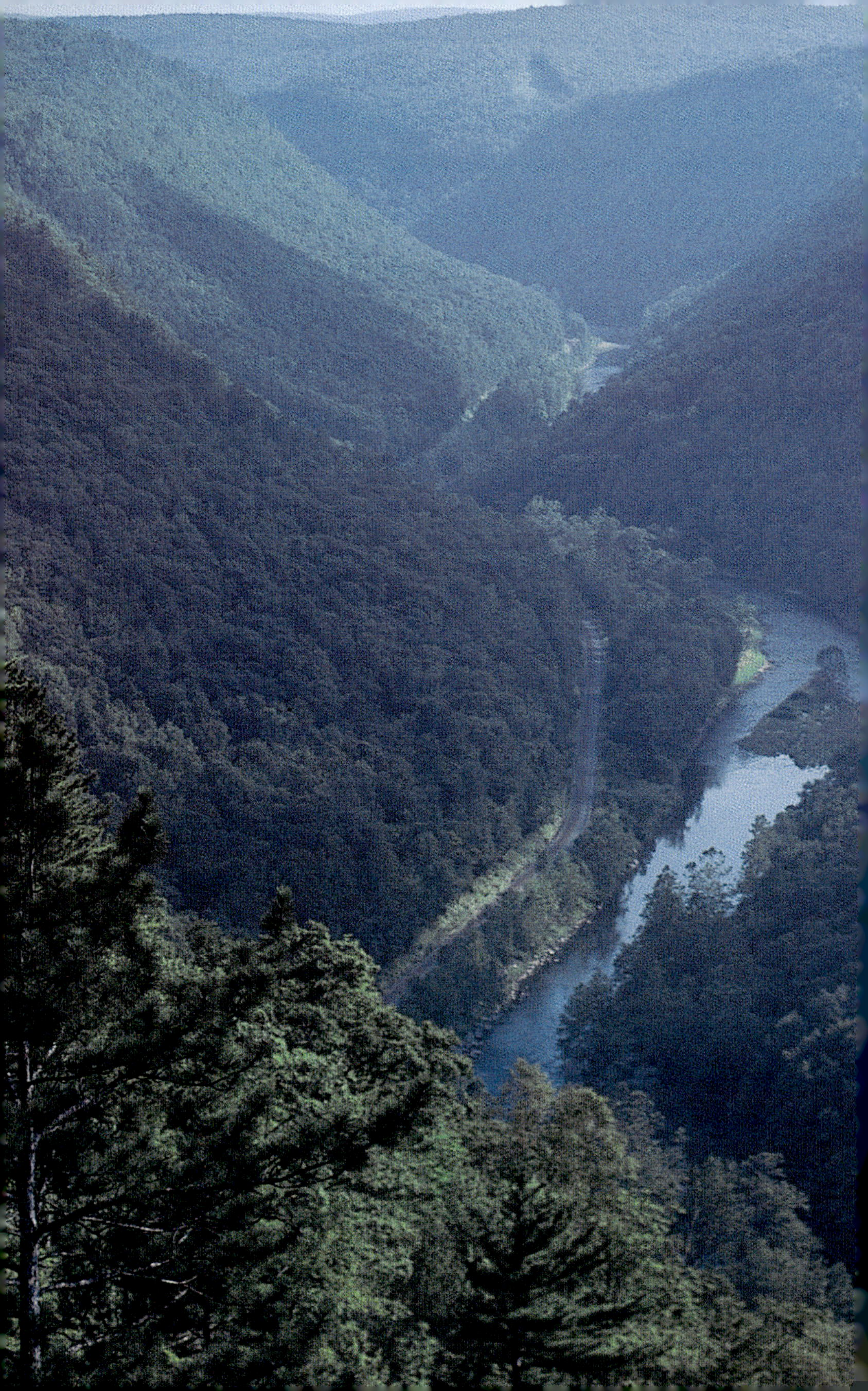

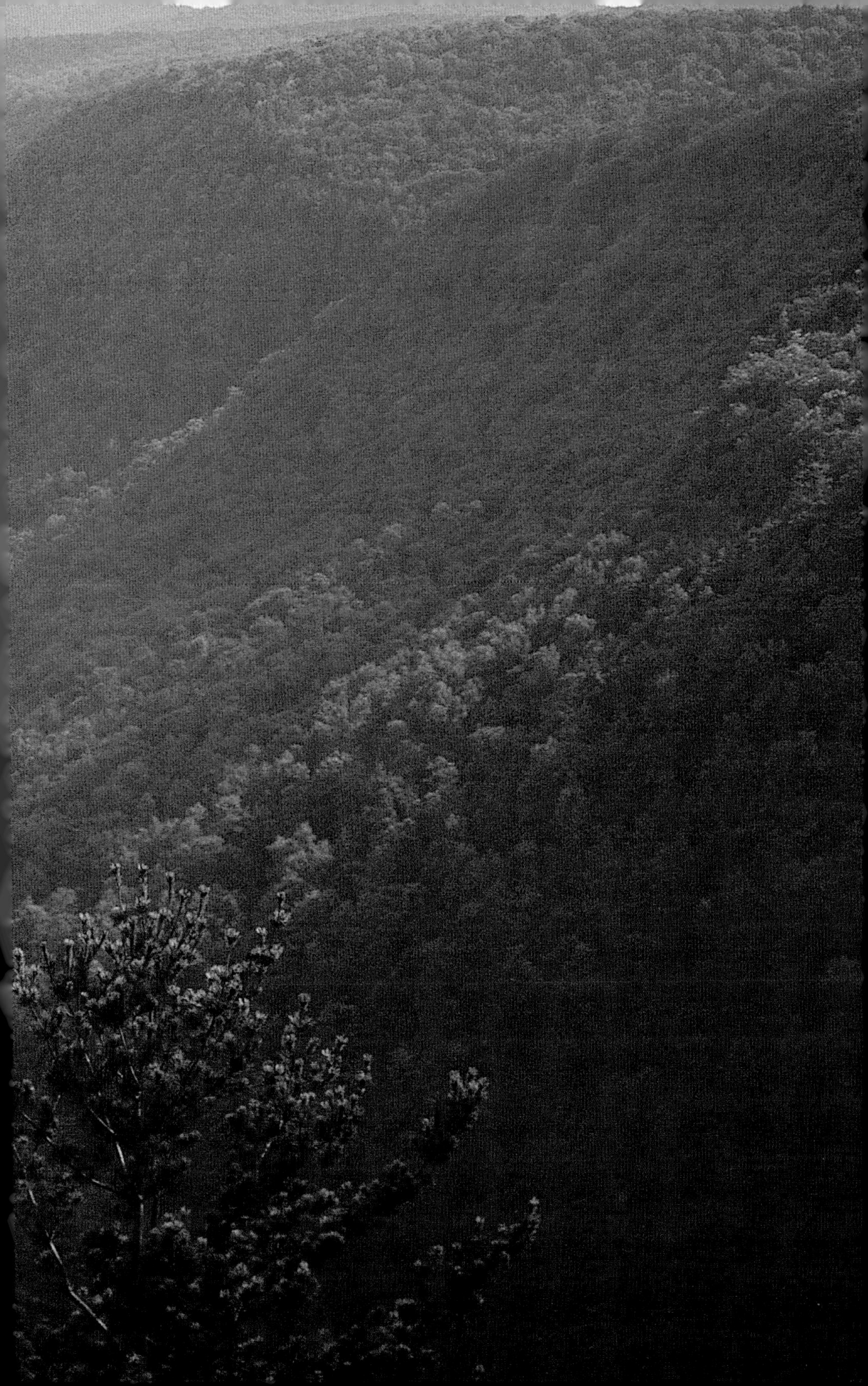

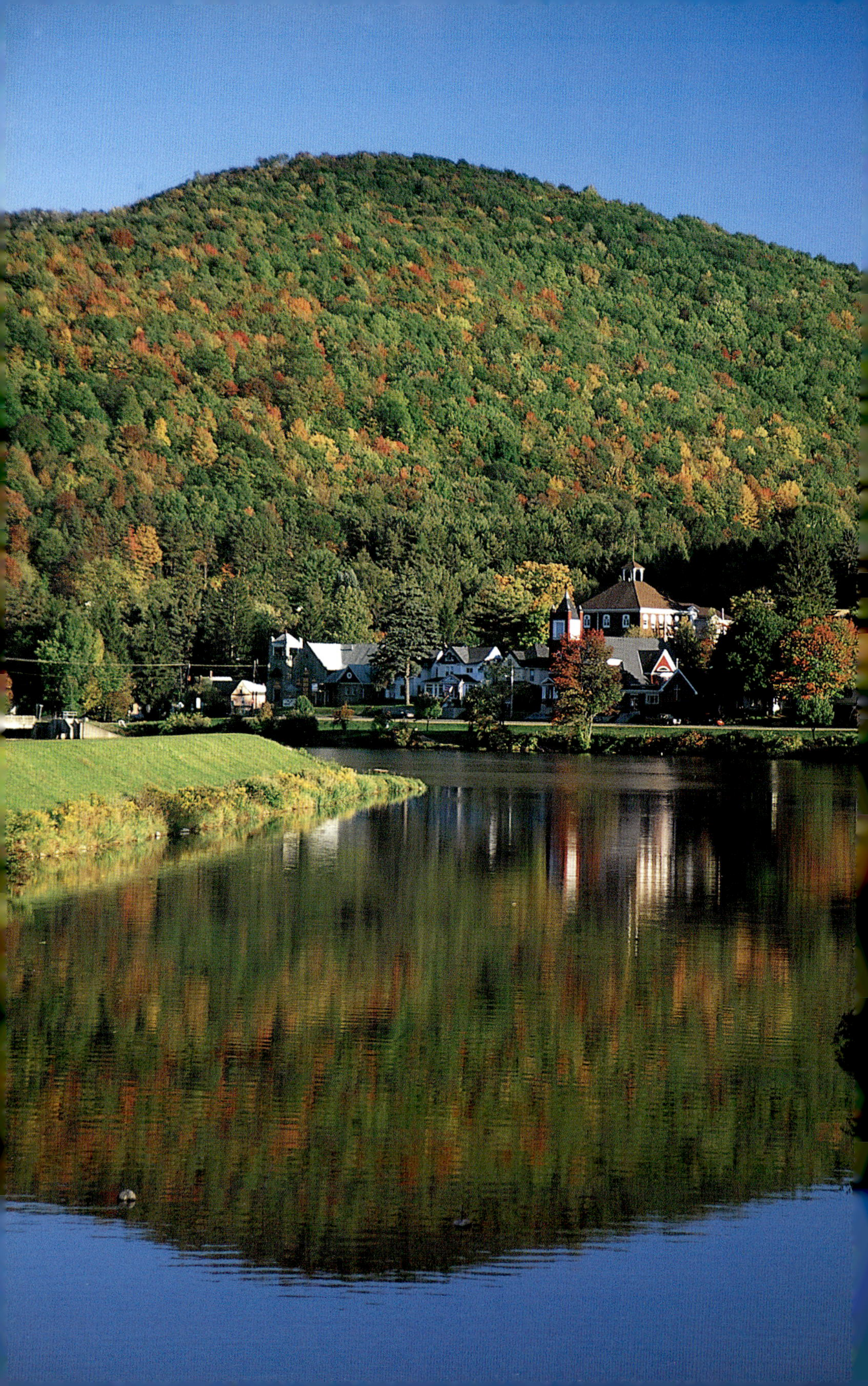

Left: **GALETON** was built during the heyday of the region's lumbering business and at one time contained numerous lumber mills, a tannery, and other businesses that were part of a boom town economy, like taverns, a hospital, an opera house, and a brewery. Today Galeton offers a "self guided tour of a lumbering town." The picturesque community also summons outdoors enthusiasts who like to hunt and fish in the area. **Above:** There are more than 2 million acres of state forest land in 48 of Pennsylvania's 67 counties, including 365,000 areas in Potter County. State law says the state forests exist "to provide a continuous supply of timber, lumber, wood and other forest products, to protect the watersheds, conserve the water, and regulate the flow of rivers and streams of the State and to furnish opportunities for healthful recreation to the public."

Pennsylvania Lumber Museum

We often think of Pennsylvania in terms of heavy industry like steel, transportation like the railroads, and agriculture. But it takes a trip across U.S. 6 to remind us that Pennsylvania has a long and proud history in lumbering. And there's no better place to learn about that history than at the Pennsylvania Lumber Museum between Galeton and Coudersport.

Work horses prepare for log skidding at the annual Bark Peelers' Convention held every 4th of July weekend at the Pennsylvania Lumber Museum.

Fortunately, the weekend I went there was the time for the 27th annual Bark Peelers' Convention, and I was able to see and learn a lot in addition to the museum's regular exhibits.

The museum has two large galleries that contain exhibits on the logging industry in Pennsylvania and the work of the Civilian Conservation Corps. In addition to artifacts, tools, and photographs, there are dioramas, models, displays, and a small theatre with a film on the history of logging. The museum preserves and interprets the commonwealth's prosperous lumber era when, a century ago, white pine and hemlock were the wealth of the nation.

Outside the museum building is a recreated logging camp with a mess hall and kitchen, stable, blacksmith's shop, sawfiler's shack, and a huge Shay-geared logging locomotive with cars. The railroad exhibit also includes a 1910 Barnhart log loader and there's a fully-operational steam-powered sawmill with a log holding pond nearby.

The museum, which is administered by the Pennsylvania Historical and Museum Commission, has a full schedule of events and interactive programs through the tourist season, but none bigger than the Bark Peelers' Convention, which brings old machinery, wood crafts, food vendors, and competitions to the site.

I parked at Denton Hill State Park across U.S. 6 from the museum, and walked back to the museum, passing up a chance to ride on a flat-bed trailer with hay bales for seats being pulled by a tractor. One of the first things that hits you as you approach the museum grounds is the sound of chain saws and machinery. I walked past an exhibitor using a chain saw to carve a large bear out of a block of wood and into a grove of trees where several people were operating antique engines and belt-powered equipment.

Throughout the grounds there were booths with demonstrations of blacksmithing, camp cooking, shingle-making, basket-making, butter churning, and various crafts. And there were exhibits from the Game Commission, Bureau of Forestry, and other groups. In addition, over the two days there were demonstrations of log-skidding and wood-hick skills such as sawing and bark peeling, and competitions, including greased pole, tobacco spitting, frog jumping, fiddling, and birling.

A number of food booths and music from an energetic duo playing

Below: Many scenes like this await the outdoors enthusiast who ventures into the woods of the Susquehannock, Sproul, Tiadaghton, and Tioga state forests in Potter and adjoining counties. **Right:** The 42-mile **BLACK FOREST** trail starts and finishes in a pine plantation on the state forestry road near Slate Run Village in the northwest corner of Lycoming County. The name Black Forest was derived from the dense, dark virgin coniferous forests that originally covered the region. The northern gateway of the Susquehannock Trail is on U.S. Route 6 at the top of Denton Hill, near Potato City.

WELCOME TO DOWNTOWN
CARTER CAMP, PA
POPULATION '2'
STORE — CAFE
> > > > >
BED & BREAKFAST

Below: The self-described "hub of Potter County" is the **POTATO CITY COUNTRY INN** at the 2,424-foot Denton Hill Summit in Coudersport. Potato City was built in 1949 through the combined efforts of potato growers, packers, and related industries. Much credit is given to Dr. E. L. Nixon, uncle of former U.S. President Richard M. Nixon. Before it eventually became a private enterprise, Potato City was the scene of many meetings, field days, banquets, and other functions relating to the potato industry. **Right: CARTER CAMP LODGE**, Store, and Cafe, with its population of 2, is located near the junction of Pa. 44 and 144, just south of U.S. Route 6. The facility offers lodging and meals and opportunities for hunting, fishing, snowmobiling, and other outdoor pursuits.

old-timey instruments with a lot of skill and humor rounded out the event.

For someone like me who grew up in Philadelphia, lived in Pittsburgh for several years, and now lives in Harrisburg, it was an eye-opening time that introduced a way of life that I've never really thought about much.

VISITORS INFORMATION: The museum is on U.S. Route 6 between Galeton and Coudersport. Telephone: (814) 435-2652. www.lumbermuseum.org

Left: A model of a tannery is part of the exhibits in the Visitors Center at the Pennsylvania Lumber Museum. **Above:** Tracks at the Pennsylvania Lumber Museum lead to a 1912 Shay-geared logging locomotive. The museum preserves and interprets the heritage of the lumber era, when white pine and hemlock were integral parts of the nation's wealth.

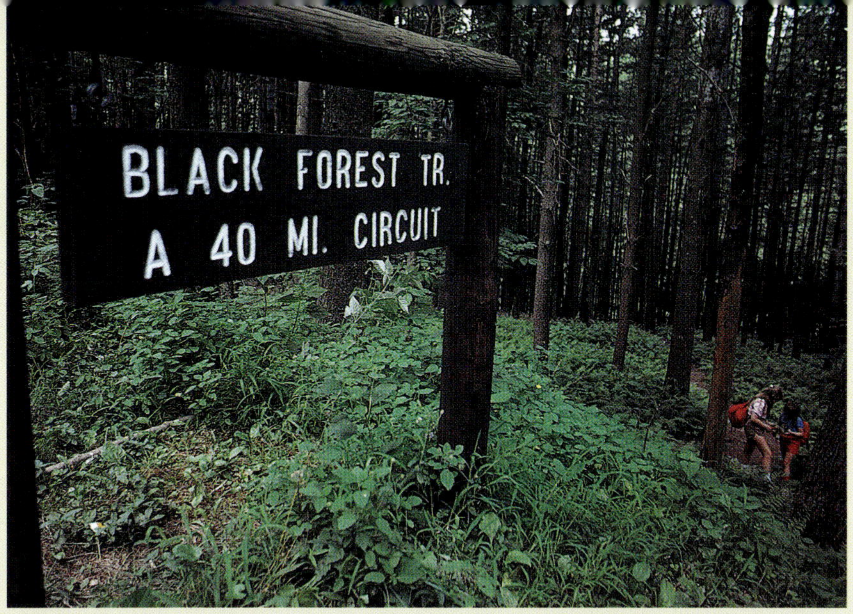
BLACK FOREST TR.
A 40 MI. CIRCUIT

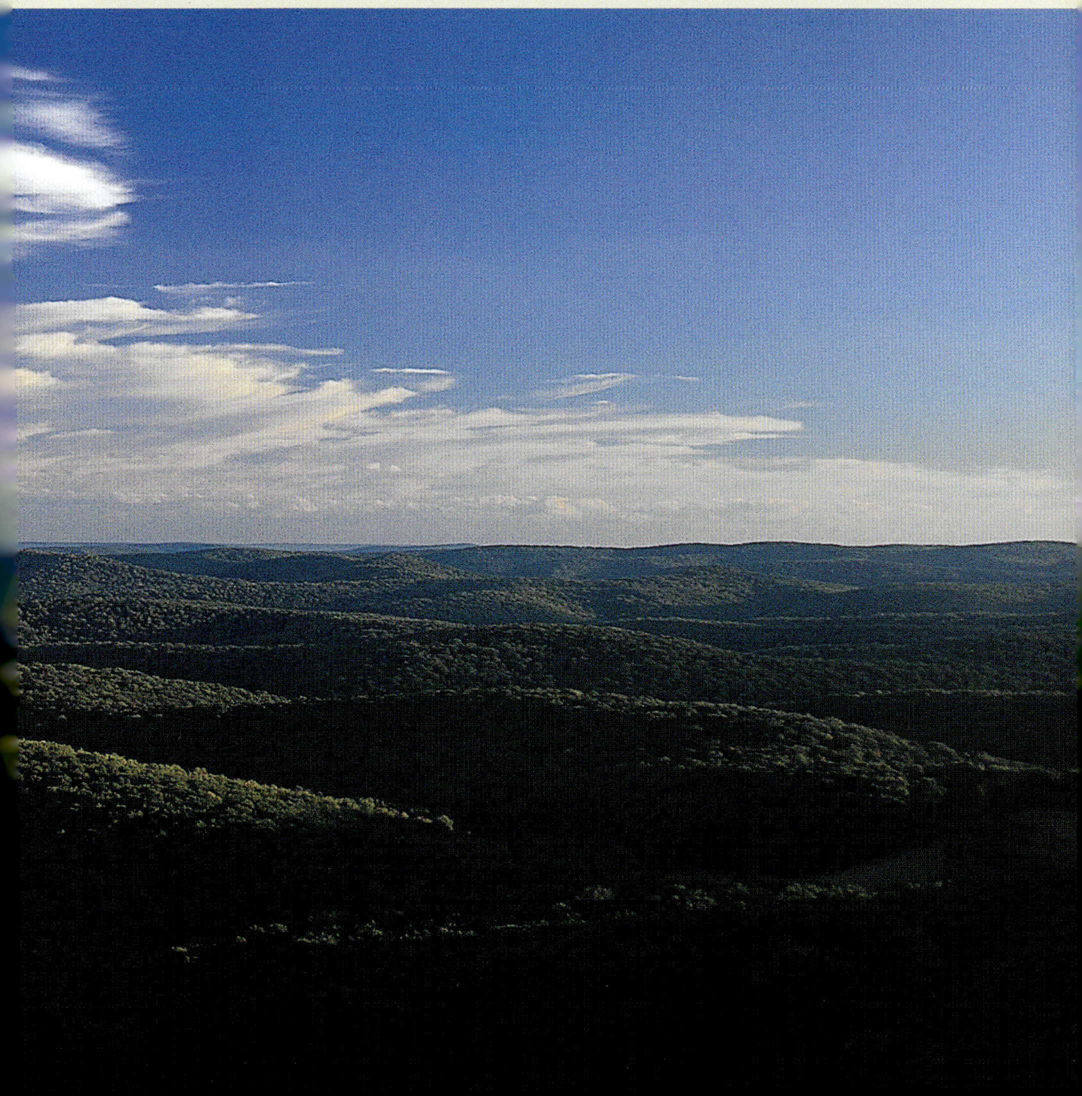

Above: John Rigas purchased his first cable TV system in **COUDERSPORT** for $300 in 1952. His Adelphia Communications, headquartered in this building, is now one of the largest cable TV companies in the country with more than 5.5 million customers in Los Angeles, southern Florida, western New York, and areas in more than 30 states, including Pennsylvania. **Below:** The Potter County Historical Society traces the history of the **COUDERSPORT** area back to 1776, when a Moravian missionary heading for Tionesta and two Indians camped in the area. The county is named for a Revolutionary War soldier who had no family connection with the area, but was deemed worthy of such recognition. The 1810 census listed only 29 residents in Potter County. Now more than 18,000 people (out of the state's 11 million) live in "God's Country." **Right:** Much of the northern tier in the western part of the state is either state or national forest land. This scene is in **KINZUA BRIDGE STATE PARK**.

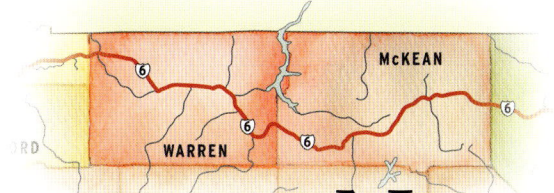

ALLEGHENY NATIONAL FOREST REGION

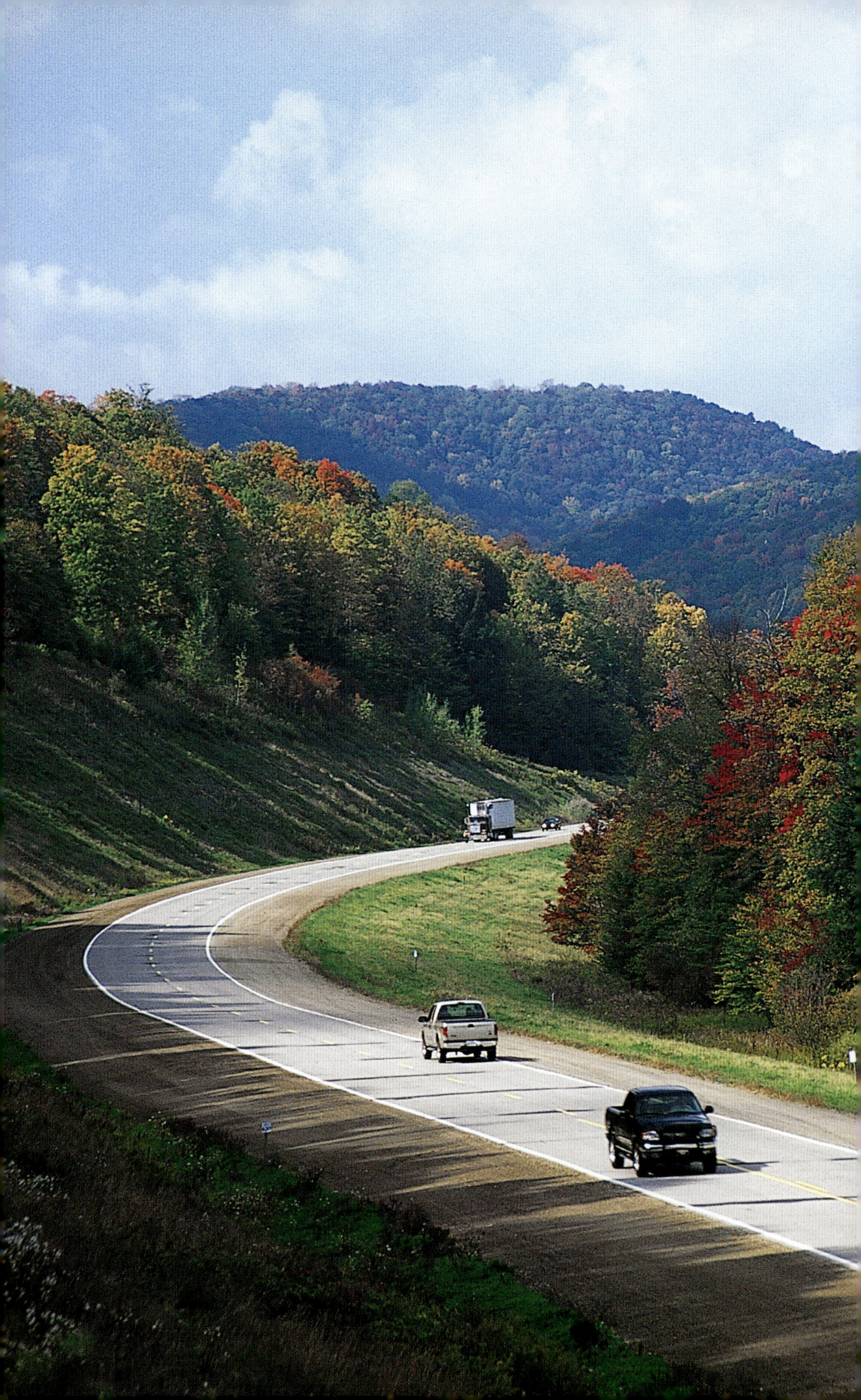

Cares fall away as travelers cross Pennsylvania on **U.S. 6**, often a two-lane highway through beautiful forest land and past striking Victorian homes. This stretch is between Galeton and Coudersport.

In 1807, the General Assembly approved Smeth's Port (now **SMETHPORT**) as the seat of justice for McKean County. Construction of the first courthouse began in 1826. The structure was rebuilt several times. This courthouse, the fourth, was built in 1946. It houses county offices and also is home to the county historical society.

America's First Christmas Store, containing four rooms with more than 10,000 gifts, is located on U.S. Route 6 in **SMETHPORT**. The site has become a magnet for bus tours from throughout the country.

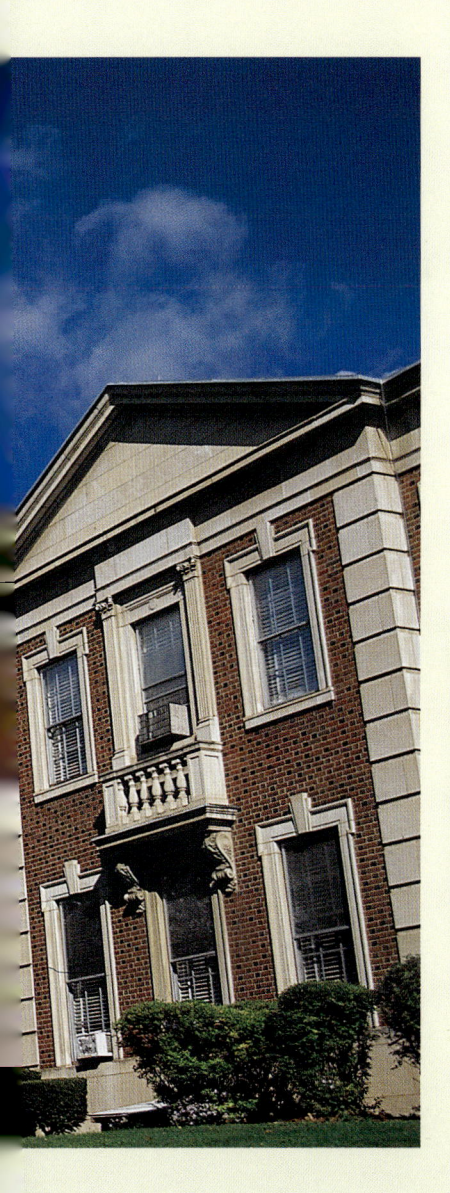

ALLEGHENY ARMS AND ARMOR MUSEUM

How many museums can you go to where you can see tanks, airplanes, and warships? Well, one is the Allegheny Arms and Armor Museum on Pa. Route 46, just a couple of miles north of U.S. Route 6 in Smethport.

The museum has more than 20 major exhibits, including armored cars, tanks, self-propelled guns, tracked recovery vehicles, armored personnel carriers, towed artillery pieces, Soviet armor, fixed and rotary wing aircraft, and a floating Coast Guard cutter.

The facility has irregular hours and the building was closed when we stopped in, but the equipment is on display in a large lot surrounding the building so we were able to see and appreciate the exhibits that have been collected there.

VISITORS INFORMATION: The museum is on Pa. Rte. 46, 2.5 miles north of Smethport. Telephone: (814) 362-2642.
www.armormuseum.com

Above Right: The Knox & Kane Railroad stops at the depot in Kane to pick up passengers and take them to the Kinzua Bridge in Kinzua Bridge State Park. Either a diesel engine or a steam locomotive pulls the train. In the park, passengers can leave the train before it crosses the bridge if they want to. Once it is on the far side of the bridge, all passengers have to get off while the locomotive is moved around to the other end.

Kinzua Viaduct

One of the themes of a visit along U.S. Route 6 is bridges. There is the Roebling Bridge in Lackawaxen, oldest wire suspension bridge in the U.S., the Tunkhannock Viaduct, and Kinzua Viaduct, which was the highest railroad bridge in the world when it was built in 1882. Today it is in Kinzua Bridge State Park (and still the second-highest railroad bridge in the world), and a walk across it provides a magnificent view of the scenic beauty of the area.

Located four miles north of U.S. 6 in Mt. Jewett, the park contains the 2,053-foot-long bridge that has been designated a National Civil Engineering Landmark. The viaduct was built as an alternative to laying an additional eight miles of track in rough terrain along the rail line leading to McKean County's coal, timber, and oil lands. Built of iron at a cost of $167,000, the original structure was 301 feet high and 2,053 feet long, and weighed 3.1 million pounds. A crew of 40 constructed the bridge in just over three months, a truly remarkable feat.

The 2,053-foot long and 301-foot tall Kinzua Viaduct has been designated a National Civil Engineering Landmark. Excursion trains from Marienville

It was rebuilt with steel in 1900 so it could accommodate heavier trains. That job was completed in 105 days by 150 men working 10-hour days. Their efforts increased its weight to 6.7 million pounds.

No trains crossed the bridge from June 21, 1959, to 1987. Now the Knox & Kane Railroad offers tourist excursions over 97 miles of track from Marienville to the park and back. The train crosses the bridge and turns around on the far side, offering a spectacular view. It stops in Kane for those who want to make a shorter (33 mile roundtrip) trip.

VISITORS INFORMATION: Kinzua Bridge State Park is reached from SR 3011 north of Mt. Jewett. Telephone: (814) 965-2646. For information on the Knox, Kane, and Kinzua excursion trains, telephone (814) 927-6621. www.knoxkanerr.com

and Kane go through the Allegheny National Forest to take visitors across the bridge.

PENN-BRAD OIL MUSEUM

While the eastern part of U.S. Route 6 teaches many lessons about anthracite coal, the western portion deals with another significant fuel source—oil. The purpose of the Penn-Brad Oil Museum in Custer City is to preserve the philosophy, spirit, and accomplishments of an oil country community, taking visitors back to the early oil boom times of the first billion dollar oil field. Volunteer guides are oil country veterans who add their personal experiences and stories to the exhibits that show how oil was brought out of the northwest Pennsylvania land.

Keystone of the exhibits is a 72'-high wooden drilling rig that is the last of between 800 and 1,000 of these rigs that were drilling in the 1880s in Pennsylvania oil fields at a time when Pennsylvania oil provided 74% of all the gas and oil used in the United States.

VISITORS INFORMATION: The Penn-Brad Oil Museum is on U.S. Rte. 219 in Custer City, three miles south of Bradford. Telephone: (814) 362-1955.
www.allegheny-vacations.com/attractions.php3

Zippo/Case Visitors Center

In 1933, George Blaisdell had an idea for a product that would meet a real need. And because he was fascinated by another recent Pennsylvania invention—the zipper—he decided to call his product Zippo. Since 1933 there have been 300 million Zippo lighters produced, each with a guarantee that if it ever does not work it will be repaired free of charge.

The story of Zippo lighters—and of Case knives, produced by W.R. Case and Sons Cutlery Company, a company that was purchased by Zippo—is told in a highly entertaining and informative way at the Zippo/Case Visitor Center in Bradford.

My wife and I took much of a week to camp in the northwest corner of the state and visit a broad range of attractions along and near U.S. Route 6. Clearly one of the highlights for both of us was the Zippo Visitor Center. The folks that developed this free attraction did it with a goal of being both informative and entertaining. And they succeeded very well.

There's a 7-by-11-foot American flag made from Zippo lighters. And there's a video screen that shows clips from various movies in which Zippo lighters were used to add dramatic effect to scenes.

Much of Zippo's history is associated with the military. During World War II, many companies had to change from producing consumer goods to producing military items. But the Zippo factory continued to make lighters, although they were exclusively for use by the military. As the company says, "Zippo lit lamps and campfires from the foxholes of Europe to the jungles of the Pacific islands. Signal fires set by Zippo lighters saved lives. Others were saved by a Zippo in pockets that caught bullets. One pilot nursed his crippled plane safely home by reading his instrument panel by the light of his Zippo. The lighter was immortalized in the columns of famous war correspondent Ernie Pyle who said of the Zippo, 'There's nothing more coveted by the GI.'"

Letters from some of the soldiers who owned Zippo lighters are on display, as are notes from those whose lighters failed because of hard use in the war. (True to the company's guarantee, the lighters were repaired free of charge at the repair center that is located in the Visitors Center and sent back to their owners.)

One of the things kids (of all ages) like about the Visitors Center is ZAC, an audiokinetic sculpture in which 20 billiard balls travel through a maze hundreds of feet long.

A small part of the center, compared to the Zippo display, is the area devoted to Case knives, a Zippo subsidiary since 1993. Case's history is portrayed and there is the Case Factory Collection, one of the most complete collections of Case knives ever assembled. One-of-a-kind factory prototypes, special issue collectible knives (including a prototype of a knife given to President Ronald Reagan) and military knives dating back to World War II are on display, along with early household cutlery and other products not currently produced by Case. A "knife-in-motion" hologram and an interactive manufacturing video complete the Case display.

Visitors Information: The Zippo/Case Visitors Center is at 1932 Zippo Drive, behind the Zippo factory, in Bradford, just off the U.S. 219 expressway. Telephone: (888) 442-1932.
www.zippo.com or www.wrcase.com

HOLGATE FACTORY TOY STORE AND MUSEUM

Tucked away on a side street in Kane, the Holgate Factory Toy Store and Museum takes visitors back to an earlier, less troubled time when toys were made of wood instead of plastic and printed circuits. The Holgate company was established in 1789 in Roxborough, which now is part of Philadelphia. Holgate Brothers produced high-quality wooden products such as handles for paint and hair brushes, tools, coffee pots, buckets that hung under Union wagons during the Civil War, soap bowls, and many other items.

The company moved to Kane in 1884 and continued its household line made from the area's hardwood timber. It started making toys in 1929, bringing in Jarvis Rockwell, the brother of famed illustrator Norman Rockwell, as chief toy designer. Many of today's toys are replicas of Rockwell's designs. One of its most important claims to fame is that it has manufactured several toys for public television's Mr. Rogers.

The small antique toy museum showcases some of Jarvis Rockwell's toys and there is a sales area where the current products, including a square yo-yo, can be purchased. At times, it is possible to watch the toys being made.

VISITORS INFORMATION: The Holgate Factory Toy Store and Museum is just off U.S. Route 6 on Wetmore Avenue in Kane. Telephone: (814) 837-7600 or (800) 499-1929 for open hours.
www.holgatetoys.com

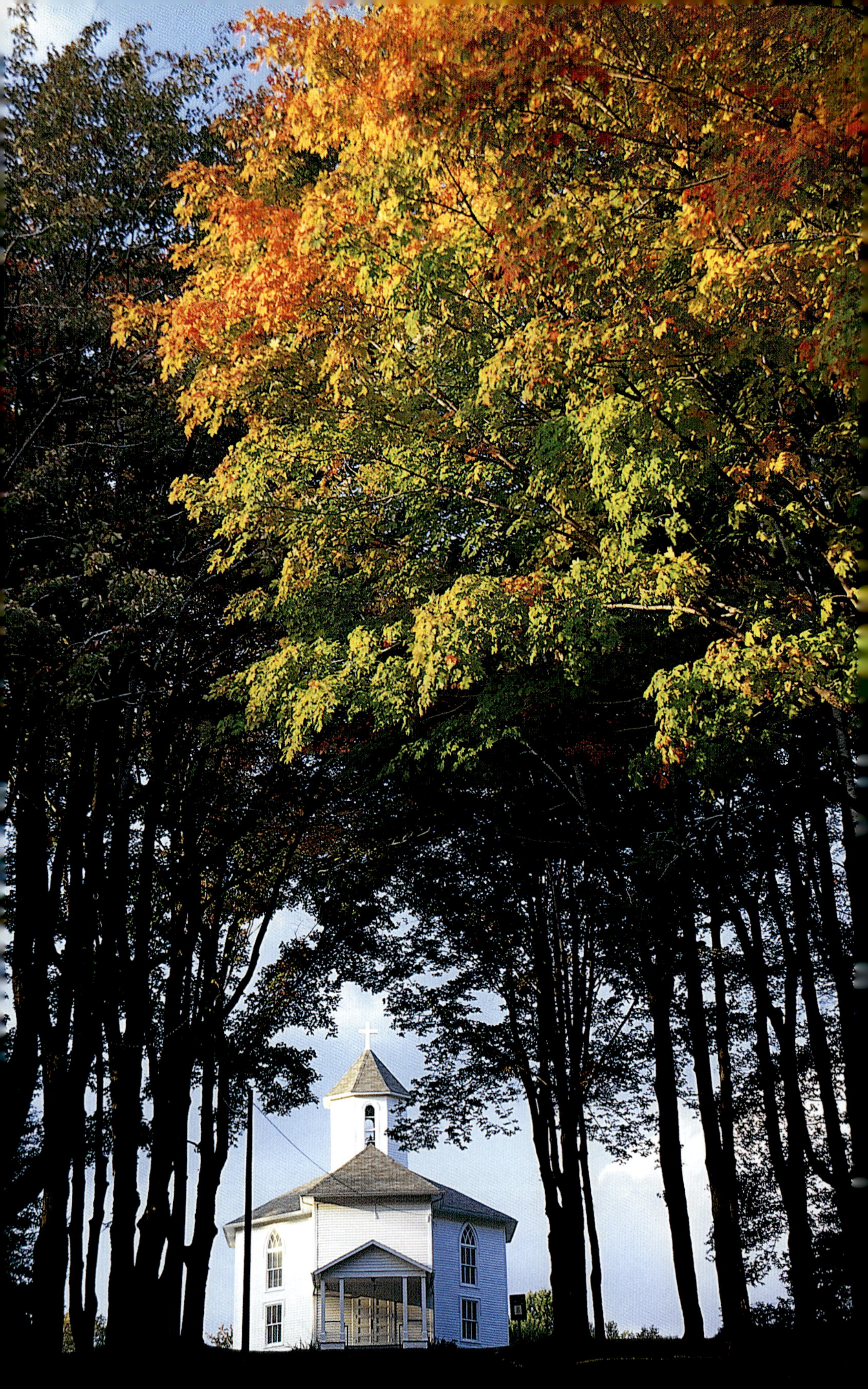

Left: In 1887, the **SWEDISH EVANGELICAL LUTHERAN NEBO CHURCH** was built on a hill near the village of Mt. Jewett. Its octagonal shape was intended to resemble a church in Stockholm, Sweden. **Above:** The **KANE MEMORIAL CHAPEL AND MUSEUM** was built from 1876 to 1878 as the First Presbyterian Church of Kane. It now is owned by the Church of Jesus Christ of Latter Day Saints and is the oldest church in the borough. The chapel retains its original stained glass windows. The vaulted ceiling is constructed of black cherry wood and there is a pipe organ in the front of the chapel. The facility houses artifacts from Civil War Gen. Thomas L. Kane, who founded the town; his brother, Arctic explorer Elisha Kane; and presidents of the U.S. and other statesmen. It also is a satellite facility for the Mormon Family History Library in Salt Lake City.

Allegheny National Forest/Kinzua Dam

For much of our trip along U.S. Route 6 in Pennsylvania, we were aware of how forested our state is. And nowhere did we feel that more than in the Allegheny National Forest. I was reminded over and over again of *Pennsylvania Tapestry: Scenes from the Air,* Blair Seitz' book of aerial photographs taken throughout Pennsylvania, and the very different view of the state that one gets from that perspective

North of Route 6, we took several smaller roads through the Allegheny National Forest to be able to see the mammoth Kinzua Dam and Allegheny Reservoir. The Forest is 513,000 acres, with more than

The Allegheny Reservoir created by the Kinzua Dam is part of a flood control system operated by the U.S. Army Corps of Engineers for the Allegheny and Upper Ohio River basins. The Big Bend Visitor Center just downstream of the dam contains slide programs, brochures, exhibits, and displays that explain and illustrate the purpose and operation of the dam, power plant, and other area features. The reservoir is at the heart of one of the most popular outdoor recreation areas in the northeast United States.

600 miles of trails, abundant wildlife, the Longhouse National Scenic Drive, and 86.8 miles of North Country National Scenic Trail.

The reservoir created by the dam is 25 miles long with more than 100 miles of shoreline. It was cool on the fall day that we were there, and no one was on the lake that we could see, but I can imagine the powerboat activity that occurs on warm days.

Great views of the lake are available from a number of scenic overlooks easily reached from the roads that traverse the area.

VISITORS INFORMATION: Allegheny National Forest is located in portions of several northwest Pennsylvania counties, with recreational facilities throughout the Forest. Telephone: (814) 723-5150 or (814) 362-4613. www.fs.fed.us/r9/allegheny

Warm weather recreational activities on the Allegheny Reservoir include boating, swimming, fishing, camping, and hiking. The area is awash with color as the leaves change in the fall, and in the winter there are ice-fishing, cross-country skiing, and snomobiling.

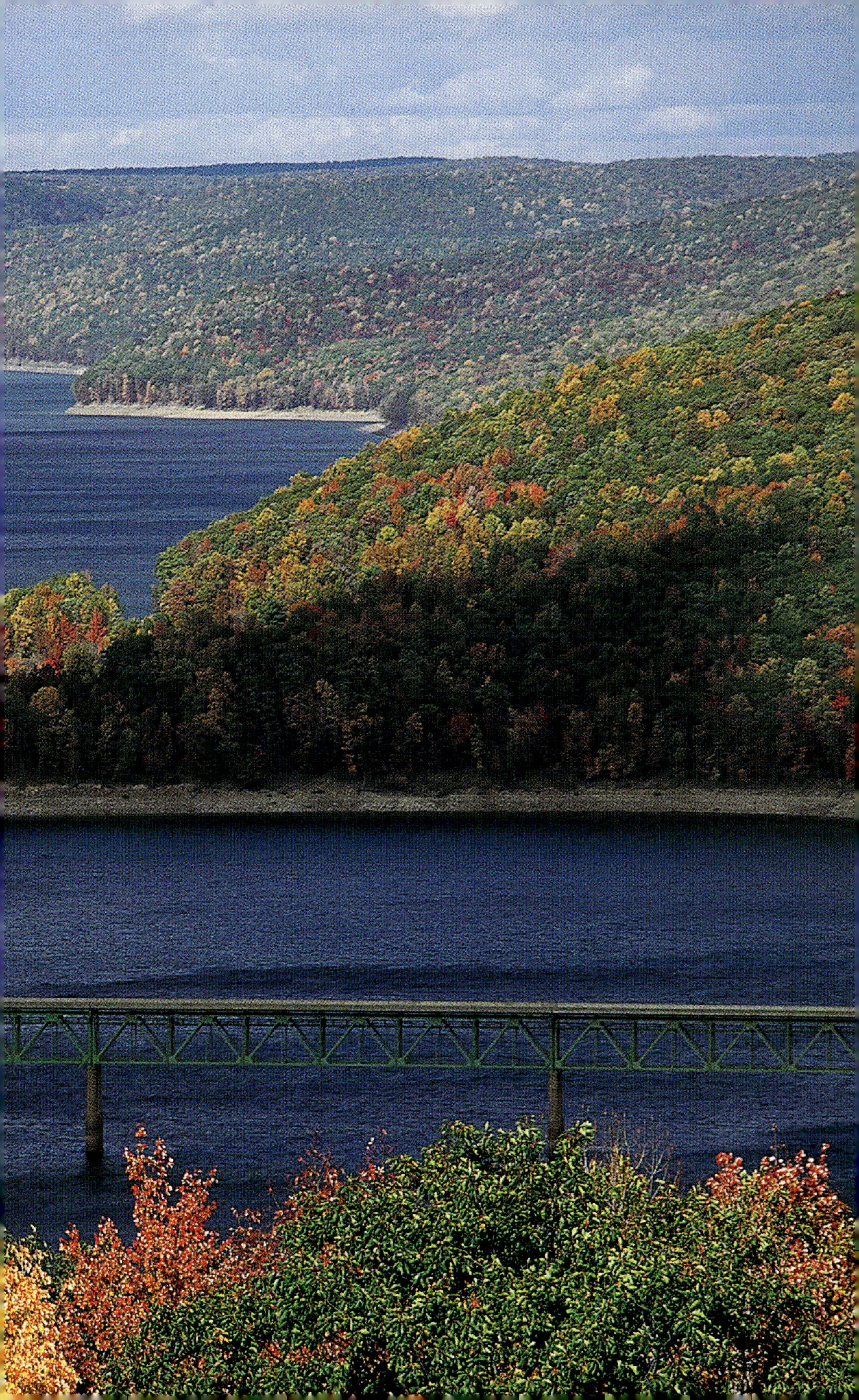

Above: Travelers learn much about America's growth and development from museums along U.S. Route 6 and also from places such as this that sell much of the old equipment that was used in the development of this country. **Right:** Warren County was created on March 12, 1800, from parts of Allegheny and Lycoming Counties and named for General Joseph Warren. It was attached to Crawford County until 1805 and then to Venango County until 1819, when it was formally organized. **WARREN**, the county seat, where this courthouse is located, was laid out in 1795 and incorporated as a borough on April 3, 1832.

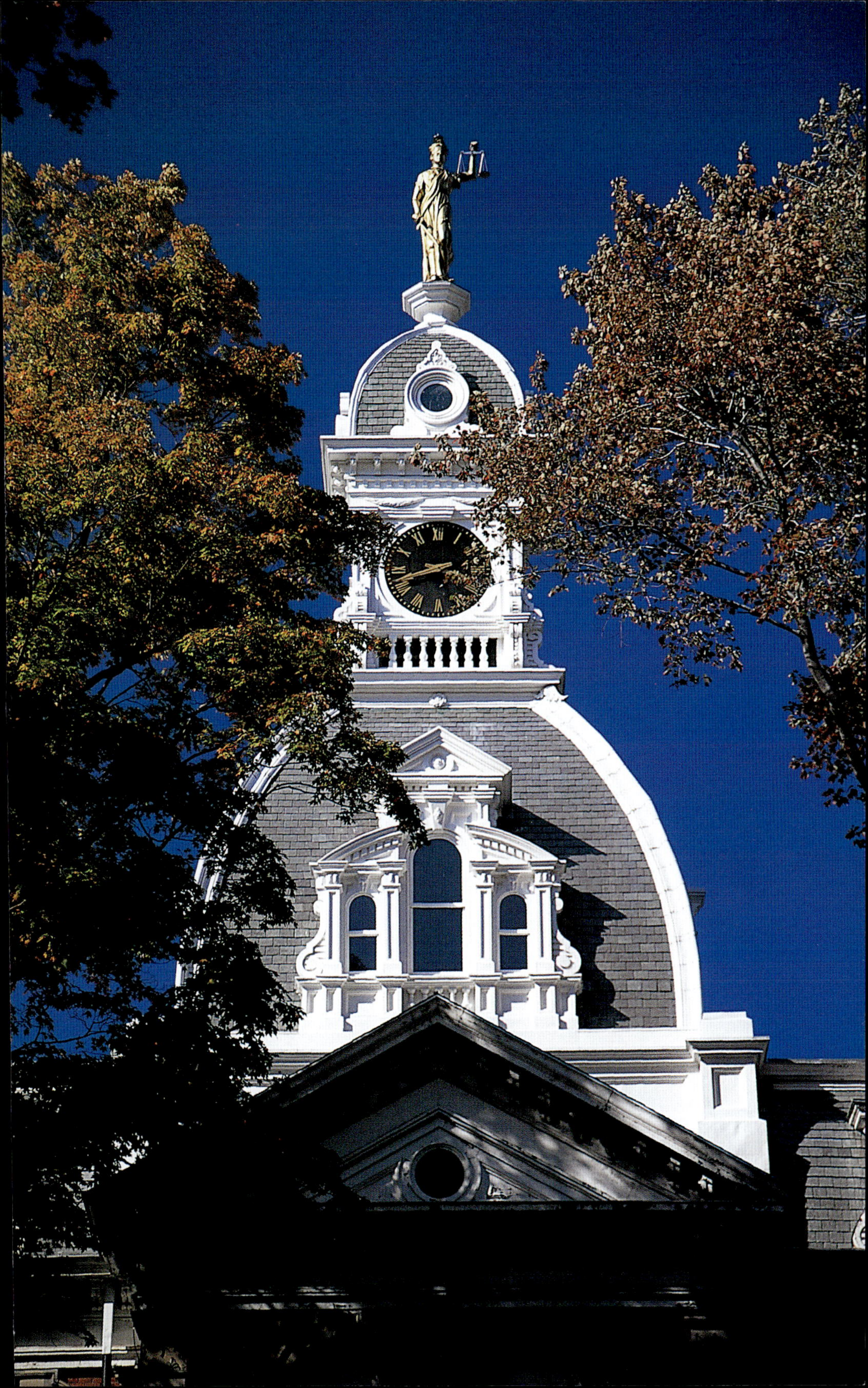

Founded by John L. Blair, Sr., as the New Process Company, **BLAIR CORP.** today sells men's and women's clothing and home products primarily through mail order. Blair started his business by selling black raincoats made with a new waterproofing process (hence the company name) to undertakers and clergymen through the mail with credit extended for a one-week free trial. The company is now the ninth largest consumer apparel catalogue store in the U.S.

The **Struthers Library Theatre** was built by Thomas Struthers in 1883. It contained a theatre, a library, and space that was rented out to various organizations. Struthers was an entrepreneur and philanthropist who founded the Struthers Wells Company. He was 80 years old when he decided to give the town of Warren a new library and included the theatre and rental space for Masonic groups and others so the building could generate income to support the library. It is the 18th oldest operating theatre in the U.S. and has been renovated for use today for summer theatre in Warren.

Erie Region

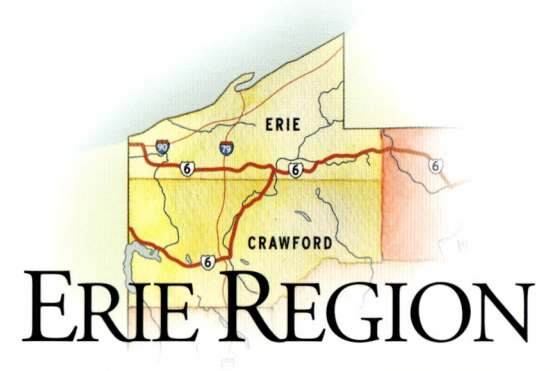

LINESVILLE SPILLWAY

How many places do you know where you can see ducks walking on the backs of fish? Not too many, I'll bet. Well one such place is the Linesville Spillway of Pymatuning Reservoir at the western end of U.S. Route 6 near the Ohio border.

At the spillway, feeding the fish is a way of life. There's even a roadside stand that sells bread visitors can use to feed the fish. There are so many fish crowding around to try to get some of the bread that ducks actually walk on their backs to try to get the bread being thrown in for themselves. Trust me on this, you have to see it to believe it. And it's worth seeing because of the beauty of Pymatuning and nearby Conneaut Lake, which is a famous summer resort area.

VISITORS INFORMATION: Follow signs to the spillway from U.S. Route 6 in Linesville.

The **RIVERSIDE INN AND HOTEL** on the banks of French Creek in Cambridge Springs has been in continuous operation since 1885, when it was built to accommodate the wishes of wealthy patrons during the mineral water boom of the late 19th century. The Riverside Inn and Hotel was perhaps the first health spa of its kind. There were many types of baths, including Russian, Turkish, cabinet, electrical, sea salt, mineral, and needle. A Vibratory for electrical treatments and an X-ray machine also were available.

In 1868, the General Assembly provided a survey and cost estimate to drain the
Pymatuning swamp and create farmland, but the plan was scrapped because
it would have crippled downstream industries in the Beaver and Shenango

valleys. A severe flood in 1913 spurred legislative action, however, and money was appropriated to build the dam that created the 17,000-acre reservoir.

Meadville Market House

It was getting to be lunchtime as we finished our short hike at the Erie National Wildlife Refuge and wanted to go on to Conneaut Lake and Linesville, so we went through Meadville and sought out the Meadville Market House, one of the state's oldest markets.

Anna and I are spoiled because we live in Harrisburg, home to the historic Broad Street Market, and also are close enough to Lancaster and

Fresh produce and local crafts and products abound at the Meadville Market House, which has been in operation since 1870. The market was renovated in 1970 and is a meeting place for people from all walks of life as well as a core structure supporting downtown Meadville.

York to visit their markets. Meadville's is an attractive brick building, smaller that the others we know, with a few craft and commercial stands, a lunch counter, and a restaurant. One advantage they have is that their market is open six days a week, while those in our area usually are only open two or three days.

We had an excellent soup and sandwich lunch at the counter inside the market house and then were back on the road.

VISITORS INFORMATION: The market house is at 910 Market Street in downtown Meadville. Telephone: (814) 336-2056.

In 1826, the **EAGLE HOTEL** was built in Waterford to handle stagecoach passengers traveling between Erie and Pittsburgh. The area declined as transportation changed, and in 1977 the Fort LeBoeuf Historical Society purchased the Eagle Hotel with plans to restore it to its former glory. It has been listed on the National Register of Historic Places and is operated today as a restaurant.

ERIE NATIONAL WILDLIFE REFUGE

A few miles outside of Meadville in Crawford County lies a natural area managed by the federal government as a haven for migratory birds. Although it is called the Erie National Wildlife Refuge, it is some 35 miles south of Lake Erie and was named for the Erie Indians, who lived in the area.

There are more than 2,500 acres of wetlands in the refuge, including beaver floodings, marshes, swamps, man-made impoundments, and creeks and wet meadows, all providing desirable waterfowl habitat. A management objective is to provide waterfowl and other migratory birds with nesting, feeding, brooding, and resting habitat. Other objectives are to provide habitat to support a diversity of other wildlife species and to enhance opportunities for wildlife-oriented public recreation and environmental education.

Grasslands are being developed near wetlands to provide dense nesting cover for ground-nesting waterfowl and other birds. A cooperative farming program permits farmers to cultivate crops on refuge lands. Farmers agree to raise certain crops such as oats, grass, clover, and corn. In return for being able to use the land, they leave the refuge a share of the crops. The refuge shares are usually left in the field as supplemental food for wildlife.

The refuge provides nesting habitat for 113 bird species and has attracted 237 species overall. There also are 47 species of mammals on the refuge, a number of kinds of fish, and 37 species of amphibians and reptiles.

There were few other people there the day we visited, and we took our two dogs and one of the cats for a walk along part of the Tsuga Nature Trail near the headquarters/visitor center building. The sun came out for a little while and it was a beautiful, serene walk. For those in close proximity, Erie National Wildlife Refuge must be a special place to visit throughout the year.

VISITORS INFORMATION: The refuge is at 11296 Wood Duck Lane, Guys Mills. Telephone (814) 789-3585.

PRESQUE ISLE STATE PARK

It was a rainy and cold September day when my wife and I toured Presque Isle State Park in Erie, but even under those circumstances the charm and beauty of that very special state park were evident.

Geologists believe that thousands of years ago what is now the City of Erie was under a giant sheet of ice called a continental glacier. As that glacier melted and moved northward, rocks, pebbles, and sand fell off and created a ridge. So much ice melted that the valley to the north of Erie became a lake. The waves of that newly-created Lake Erie deposited sand on the ridge and created Presque Isle.

Today, Presque Isle State Park is a 3,200-acre sandy peninsula that curls out into Lake Erie. The road system within the park forms a loop that runs some 13 miles. The neck of the peninsula is attached to the mainland four miles west of downtown Erie. The park creates Presque Isle Bay, a wide and deep harbor for Erie, an important Great Lakes shipping port.

Presque Isle is a designated National Natural Landmark. Because of its many unique habitats, it has a greater number of the state's endangered, threatened, and rare species than any other area of comparable size in the state.

But the park is best known for its recreational opportunities. As the state's only "seashore," it attracts millions of visitors each summer to its sandy beaches and rolling waves. There also are facilities for boating, fishing, biking, hiking, and in-line skating.

We took our RV around the loop drive, stopping at some of the beaches and scenic overlooks, and picturing what the place must be like during the summer season.

Above: This 57-foot lighthouse was first built on Presque Isle in 1872 and lit in 1873. The red brick building at the base is used as a state park residence. The U.S. Coast Guard still maintains the flashing white light. There is an educational exhibit adjacent to the lighthouse. **Next Pages**: Geologists believe that a continental glacier covered what is now the city of Erie 11,000 years ago. As the ice melted and retreated to the north, rocks, pebbles, and sand created a ridge called a "moraine." So much ice melted that the valley to the north of Erie became a lake. The waves from Lake Erie deposited sand on the moraine and created Presque Isle, a recurring sand spit that juts seven miles out into the lake. The state park on Presque Isle has the only surf beaches in Pennsylvania.

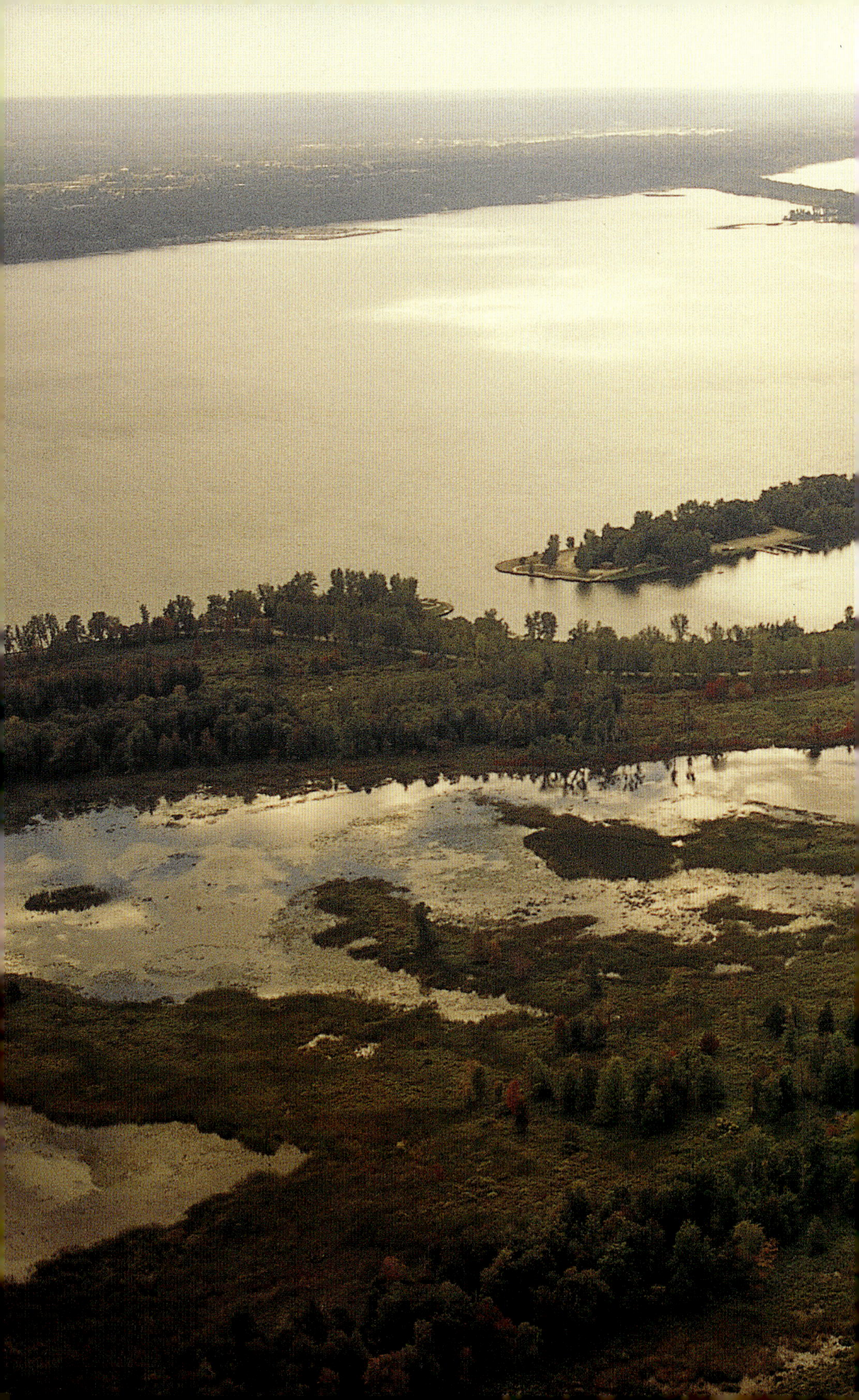

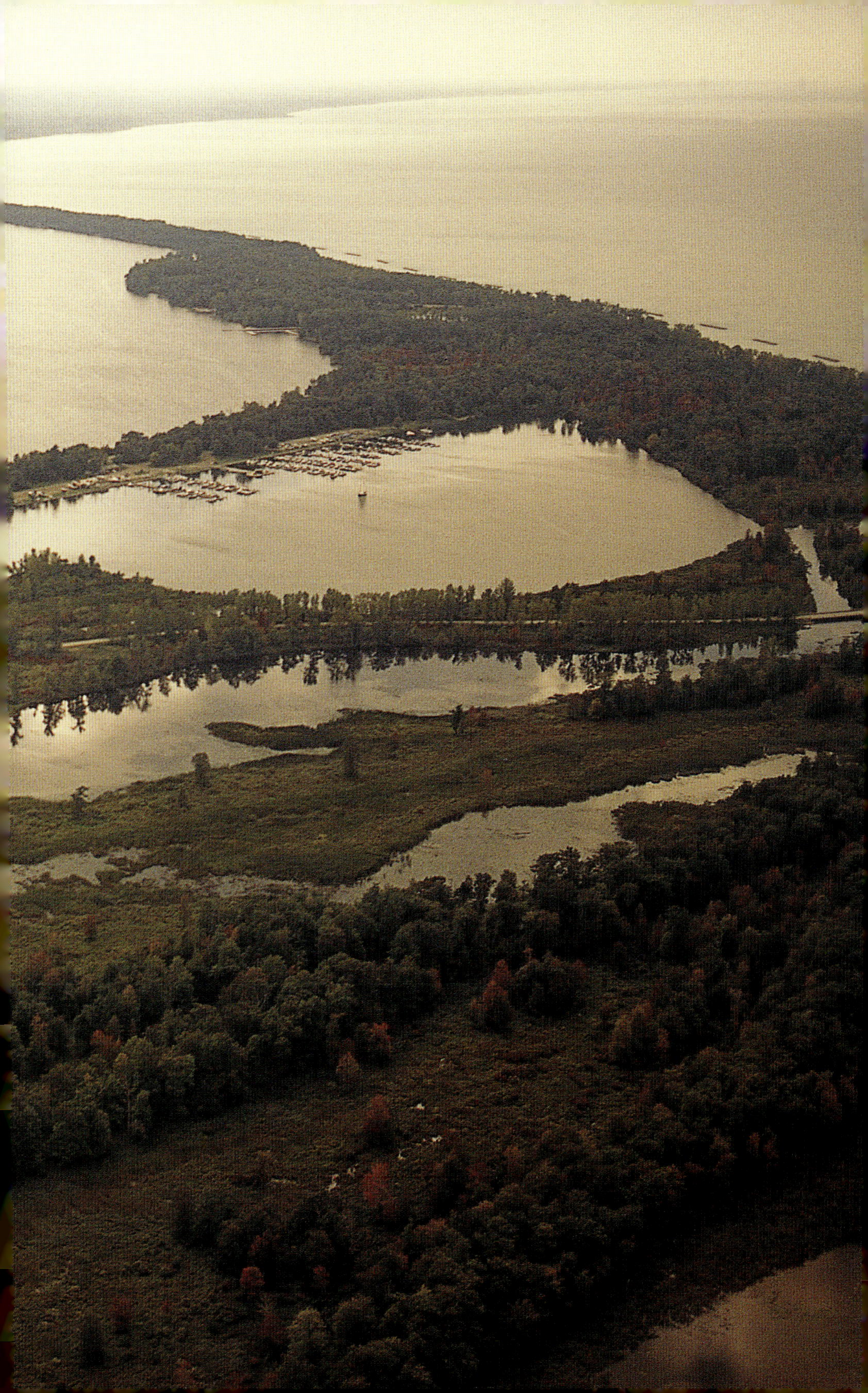

At Crystal Point is a monument to Oliver Hazard Perry, who commanded a fleet of ships at Little Bay during the War of 1812. On September 10, 1813, at the Battle of Lake Erie, Commodore Perry and his men defeated the British at Put-in-Bay near Sandusky, Ohio. After the battle, Perry and his men returned to Presque Isle to repair their ships and seek medical help for the wounded. The Perry Monument was built in 1926 to commemorate this significant battle.

On the other side of the peninsula is Presque Isle lighthouse, built in 1872 and first lit on July 12, 1873. The red brick dwelling at the base is now used as a park residence. The light is still maintained by the U.S. Coast Guard.

The park has been rated by *Birder's World* magazine as one of the best birding spots in the country. Its location on what is known as the Atlantic Flyway makes it a favorable spot for birds to stop to feed and rest on their migration across Lake Erie. Waterfowl migration occurs in March and late November through December. Shorebird migration peaks in April and September. Warbler migration is observed in mid-May and September. More than 300 different species of birds have been identified on the peninsula. A lot of information about the park and its natural history, including a bird checklist, is available at the Stull Interpretive Center near Barracks Beach.

VISITORS INFORMATION: The park entrance is reachable from Pa. Rte. 832 near the lakefront, west of downtown Erie. Telephone: (814) 833-7424.

Right: Galleries at the Erie Maritime Museum tell the story of Niagara as the reconstructed flagship of Pennsylvania and the warship that won the Battle of Lake Erie in the War of 1812.

Erie Maritime Museum

On a cool and rainy day, my wife and I steered our RV into downtown Erie to tour the Erie Maritime Museum and the Flagship Niagara, which is based at the museum. The complex is leading the renaissance of Erie's Bayfront District, joined by shops, restaurants, and other points of interest just a few miles east along the bayfront from Presque Isle State Park.

The museum was developed by the Pennsylvania Historical and Museum Commission to house a variety of interactive exhibits on the city's role in the construction of the U.S. fleet for the Battle of Lake Erie in the War of 1812, as well as the city's role as a leading center of commerce and tourism, and to provide a home for its official flagship, U.S. Brig Niagara.

The U.S. Brig Niagara is a square-rigged, two-masted warship originally armed with 18 carronades and two long guns. The restoration now berthed at the Erie Maritime Museum has a few timbers recovered from the original brig that was scuttled off Presque Isle in 1813. (photo courtesy of Erie Maritime Museum)

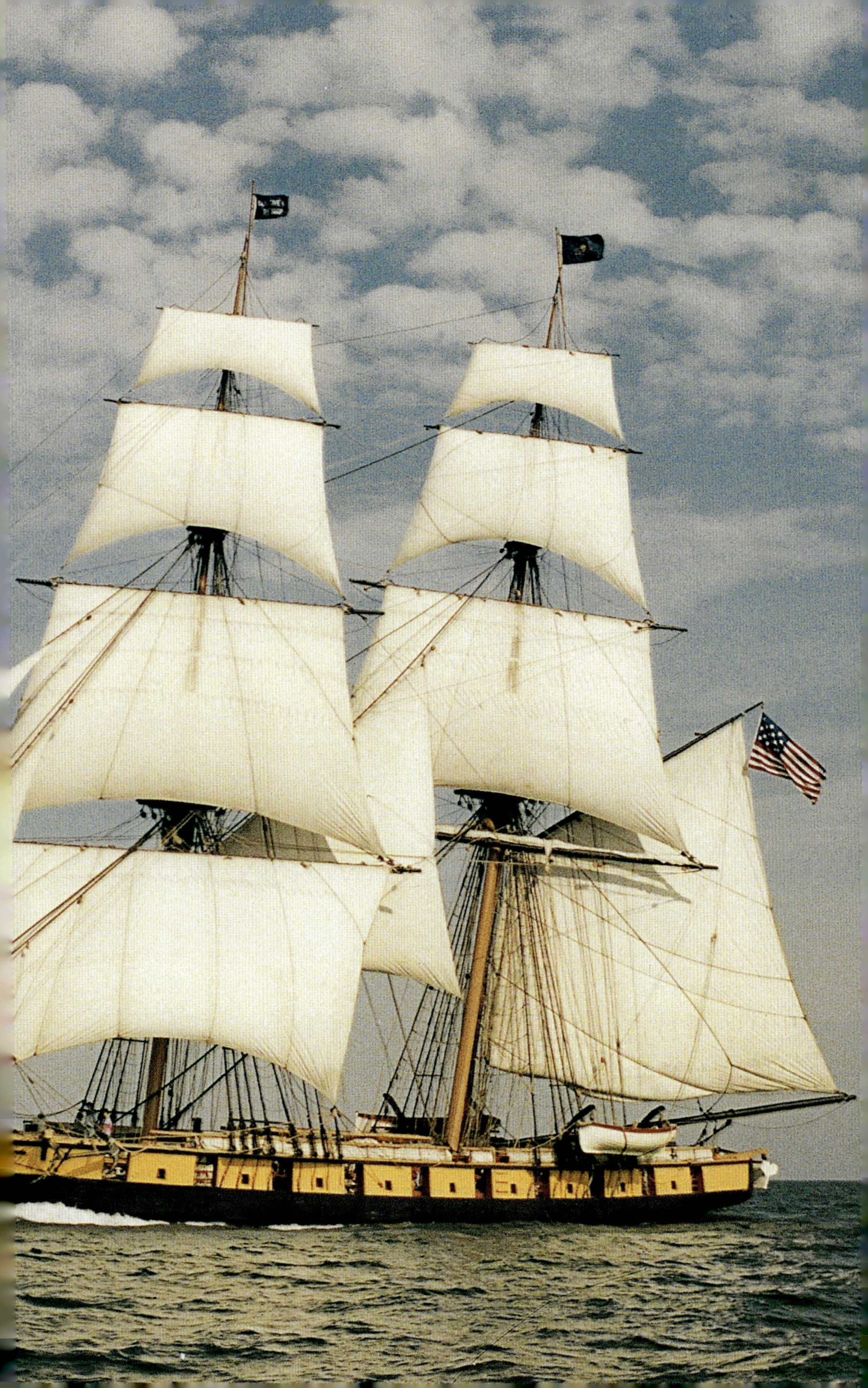

Volunteers provide guide service, an excellent way to better understand what Erie has meant to the northwestern part of the state and, truly, to all of Pennsylvania and the United States.

For those of us not from the area, it is a surprise to learn that Erie is the second largest builder of railroad locomotives, plays a key role in electrical power generation, attracts many visitors now as a summer resort destination, and is a large-scale commercial and recreational fishery.

But certainly the centerpiece of the museum's exhibits are those that depict the Battle of Lake Erie during what has been described as America's forgotten war, the War of 1812. This is one of the Pennsylvania Historical and Museum Commission's most modern museums, and it makes excellent use of the contemporary interactive techniques that are the mark of a new museum. There is a video that puts the Battle of Lake Erie into context and a full-scale reconstruction of one side of the *Lawrence*, Commodore Oliver Hazard Perry's original flagship, which actually was taken to the National Guard base at Indiantown Gap, near Harrisburg, and fired on with period cannon so visitors could see the effect of such shelling on a wooden ship.

Historical artifacts, photographs, video footage, hands-on knot and sail exhibits, and other items all come together to tell the story of the battle and the larger tale of square-rigged wooden ships, the reconstruction and sailing of the current Niagara, and Erie's more recent maritime heritage.

We learned from our guide that Perry was a "militant Quaker." As long-time members of the Quaker meeting in Harrisburg, this description sounded like an oxymoron to us, although we know that there have been Quakers who, in good conscience, have felt the need to fight on behalf of their country.

The United States declared war on Great Britain on June 12, 1812, as a result of long-simmering disputes with that country. The central dispute surrounded the kidnapping of American soldiers by the British. The British had previously attacked the USS Chesapeake and nearly caused a war two year earlier. In addition, disputes continued with Great Britain over the Northwest Territories and the border with Canada.

Finally, the attempts of Great Britain to impose a blockade on France during the Napoleonic Wars were a constant source of conflict with the United States.

On September 10, 1813, nine small ships defeated a British squadron of six vessels in the Battle of Lake Erie. This pivotal event in the War of 1812 secured the Northwest Territory, opened supply lines, and lifted the nation's morale.

Six vessels in Perry's Fleet, including Niagara, were constructed in Erie. Building of the American squadron was a remarkable feat, given Erie's mere 500 inhabitants and remote location. Shipwrights, blockmakers, blacksmiths, caulkers, boat builders, and laborers were recruited from Pittsburgh, Philadelphia, and elsewhere. Materials to construct the vessels were imported from other regions of Pennsylvania, including iron from Meadville and Pittsburgh; canvas for sails from Philadelphia; rigging, cannon shot and anchors crafted in Pittsburgh. The cannon

The Maritime Museum displays American marine artist Julian Davidson's 1887 portrait of Commodore Oliver Hazard Perry aboard Niagara.

were brought from Washington, D.C., and Sacketts Harbor N.Y. Because there were no sawmills, the lumber had to be cut, hewed, and squared by hand. In March 1813, Commodore Oliver Hazard Perry took command. By late July, Perry completed the vessels and raised volunteers to augment his sailors. A significant number of the skilled sailors were free blacks; many landsmen and soldiers were also enlisted due to a shortage of men.

On September 10, the British under Commodore Robert Heriot Barclay and the Americans under Perry met in battle near Put-in-Bay, Ohio. Perry's flagship Lawrence engaged her counterpart, while Niagara, for unknown reasons, did not close the enemy. Nevertheless, the Lawrence held fast and continued a heavy bombardment. After she was completely disabled, with most of her crew wounded or killed, Perry transferred by boat to the undamaged Niagara, sailed her into close action, broke the British battle line, and forced Barclay to surrender. In the aftermath, Commodore Perry wrote his famous report to General William Henry Harrison: " We have met the enemy and they are ours: two ships, two brigs, one schooner, and one sloop."

After the war, Niagara served as a station ship in Erie until 1820, then was scuttled there in Misery Bay, off Presque Isle State Park. To celebrate the centennial of the battle in 1913, Erie citizens raised the hulk and rebuilt her, using many of the old timbers. Niagara, towed by the USS Wolverine, visited Great Lakes ports and participated in ceremonies at Put-in-Bay on September 10, 1913. Following the commemoration, Niagara returned to Erie. In 1931, the state took custody of her and began a major restoration that was delayed by the Great Depression. Her hull was completed in 1943; masts and rigging were finally installed in 1963. By the early 1980s the Niagara was again severely decayed. The International Historic Watercraft Society was contracted to design and build a reconstruction of the Niagara. The present ship is a new vessel, incorporating both known and conjectural design features. Some original timber was installed in non-structural places.

One of the most striking exhibits at the Maritime Museum shows a replica of the U.S. Brig Lawrence, Commondore Oliver Hazard Perry's original flag ship, that was blasted with live ammunition from the Niagara's carronades to demonstrate the effect of cannon shelling on wooden ships and their crews.

On September 10, 1988, the Niagara was launched in Erie ceremonies marking the 175th anniversary of the Battle of Lake Erie and the ensuing peace between the United Kingdom and the United States.

After we had finished with the museum exhibits on the guided tour, we went outside to board the Niagara. We were struck by how small it seems and how uncomfortable serving on board it could have been. The cabins and common areas below deck are small and cramped with low ceilings that can whack the unsuspecting or careless on the head.

But even tied to the dock, you get a sense of the exhilarating freedom and pure joy that must come when she is underway under full sail.

VISITORS INFORMATION: The museum and Niagara are located at 150 E. Front Street, Erie. Telephone: (814) 452-2744. www.brigniagara.com

Below: Completed in 1839 as the Erie branch of the U.S. Bank of Pennsylvania, the **ERIE ART MUSEUM** building downtown in Discovery Square is more commonly called the Old Customs House. The Greek Revival building houses galleries, offices, classrooms, and collections. On display is Erie native Lisa

Lichtenfels' Avalon Restaurant, described by the artist as a "frozen moment in the life of the now defunct downtown diner." The tableau, that took more than a year to complete, has 21 soft-sculpture figures scaled to one-third size. **Next Pages:** Marina docks in E R I E are home to many pleasure boats that ply the lake.

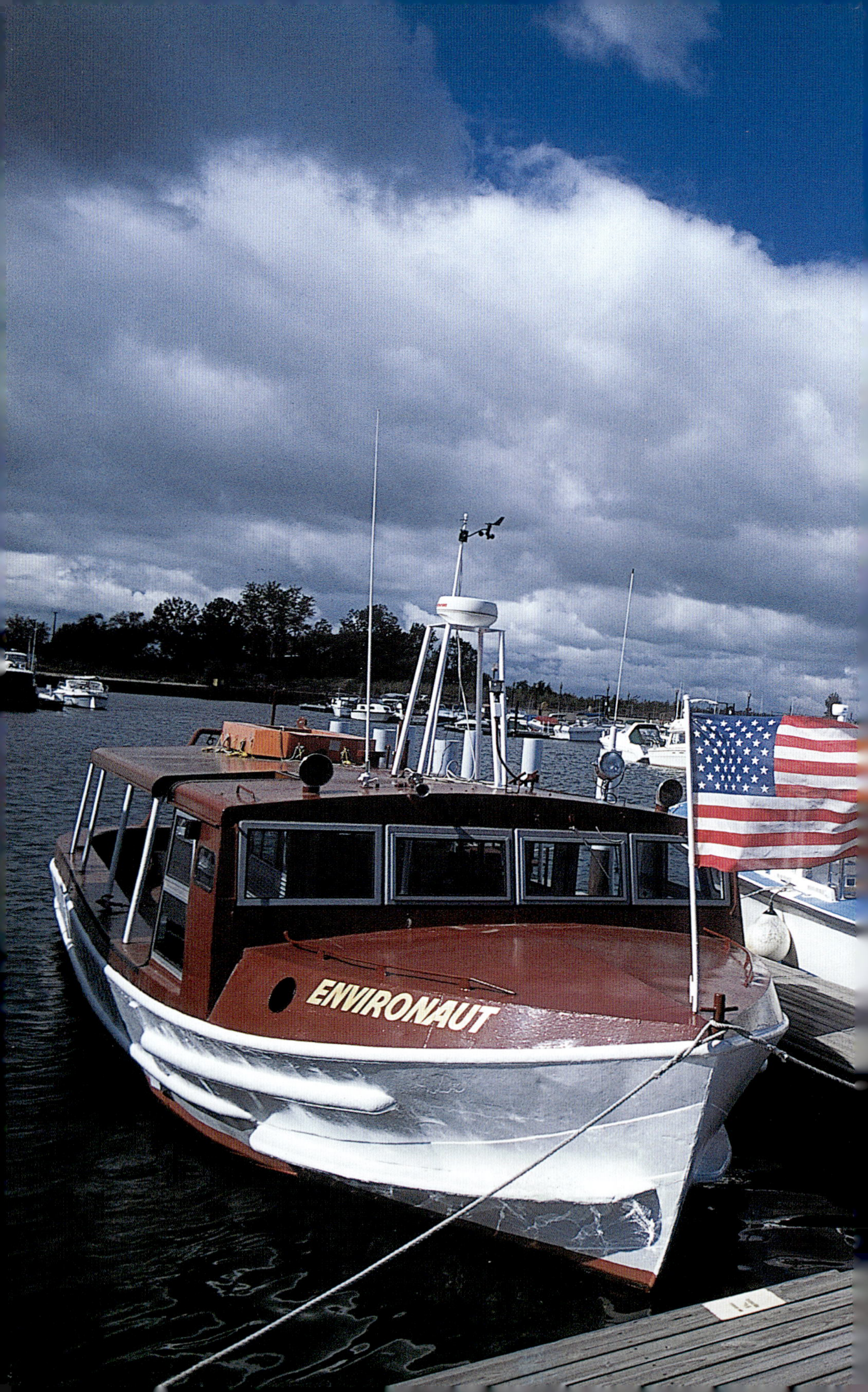
ENVIRONAUT
14

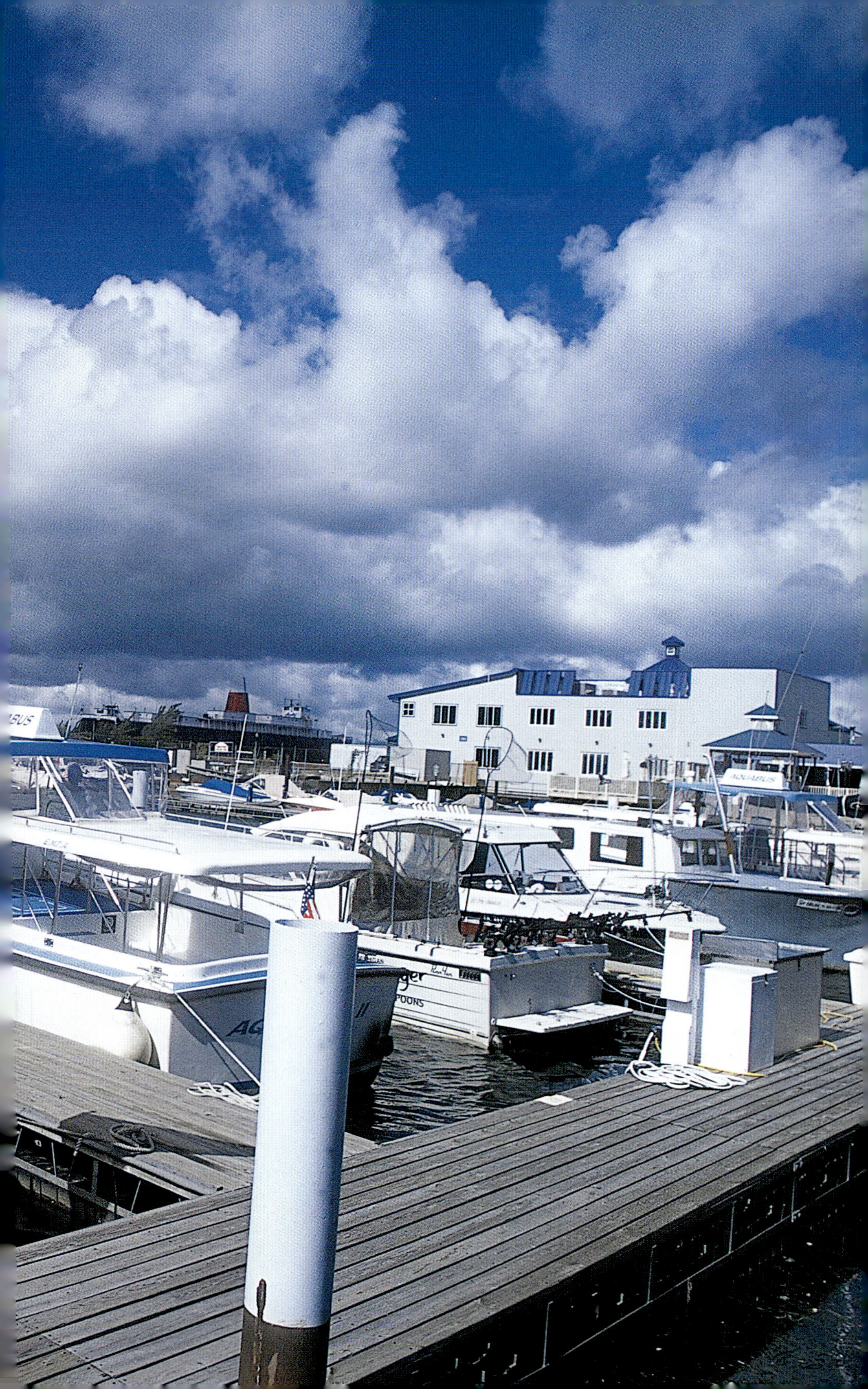
AQUABUS

INDEX

Page numbers of photographs are in **bold type.**

Adelphia Communications, 92
Allegheny Arms and Armor Museum, 98
Allegheny National Forest, 108-11
Allegheny Reservoir, **108-11**
Alpine Inn, **37**
America's First Christmas Store, **97**
anthracite. *See* coal industry
aqueducts. *See* bridges
arts festivals, 15, 35

Barclay, Robert Heriot, 134
Bark Peelers' Convention.
 See Pennsylvania Lumber Museum
Battle of Lake Erie, 128-35
bed-and-breakfasts. *See* inns
biking. *See* outdoor recreation
birding. *See* outdoor recreation
Black Forest Trail, 90-**1**
Blair Corporation, **114**
Blair, John L., Sr., 114
Blaisdell, George, 103
boating, 22, **30-1**, **71**, 78-9,
 124, **138-9**. *See also* outdoor recreation
Bradford, 102-4
Bradford County Courthouse
 and Historical Museum, **68**
Bradford County Regional
 Arts Council, 68
bridges, 24-**5**, 56-**7**, **70**, 99-**101**
Buchanan, James, 67
Burlington, 70

Cambridge Springs, 117
canals, 24, 33, 36, 63
canoeing. *See* boating
Carbondale, **39**
Carriage House Antiques, **54**
Carter Camp Lodge, 88-**9**
Case knives, 103-4
churches, 39, **70**, **106-7**
Civil War, 52, 107

Civilian Conservation Corps, 85-6
Clarks Summit, 54, 57
coal industry, 24, 46-8, 49-**50**
Cohen, A. Burton, 56
Colton Point State Park, 79
Columns, The, 15, **17**
Conneaut Lake, 117, 120
conservation, 18-9, 62, 85-6
Coudersport, 84-8, **92**, 95
courthouses, **38**-9, **68**, 74-**5**, **96**, 112-**3**
covered bridge, **70**
crafts demonstrations, 67, 86
Custer City, 98, 102

Davidson, Julia, 133
Delaware and Hudson Canal,
 24-5, 33, 36
Delaware Aqueduct, 24-**5**
Delaware, Lackawanna, and
 Western Railroad, 44, 51, 56
Delaware River, **22**-29
Denton Hill State Park, 86
Dorflinger, Christian, 34-5
Dorflinger Glass Museum, **14**, **34-35**
Dorflinger-Suydam Wildlife
 Sanctuary, **14**-15, 34-**5**

Eagle Hotel, **122**
Electric City Trolley Station
 and Museum, 40-**42**
Erie, 124, 128-37
Erie Art Museum, 136-7
Erie Maritime Museum, **129-35**
Erie National Wildlife Refuge, 120
Everhart, Isaiah Fawkes, 52
Everhart Museum of Natural
 History, **52-3**

Falls Port Inn, **32-3**
fine arts. *See* museums
fishing, 22, 26, 83, 88, 110,

140

124, 132. *See also* outdoor recreation
forests. *See* Allegheny National Forest,
Pennsylvania State Forests & Parks
forestry. *See* lumber industry
Fort LeBeouf Historical Society, 122
Foster, Stephen, 70
French Azilum, **64-7**
French Revolution, 64-7

Galeton, **82**-4, 95
Girard, Stephen, 64
glassmaking, 34
Grand Army of the Republic
  Highway. *See* U.S. Route 6
Grand Canyon of Pennsylvania, **78-81**
Greenpoint Flint Glass Works, 34
Grey, Lina (Dolly), 27-9
Grey Towers, **18-21**
Grey, Zane, 26-9
*Guide to the State Historical
  Markers of Pennsylvania,* 5
Guys Mills, 123

Hale's Opera House. *See*
  Keystone Theatre
Hallstead, 57
Hawley, 29, 33
Hawley, Irad, 33
hiking. See outdoor recreation
Hill, William, 77
historical societies, 15, 92, 96, 122
Holgate Factory Toy Store
  and Museum, 105
Hone, Philip, 36
Honesdale, 35, **36-7**
hotels, 51, **59**, **122**. *See also* inns
Hunt, Richard Morris, 18

Immigration, 46
Indians. *See* Native Americans
inns, **32-3**, **37**, **69**, **88-9**, **116-**7.
  See also hotels
International Historic
  Watercraft Society, 134

Kane, 98-101, 105, 107
Kane, Elisha, 107
Kane Memorial Chapel and Museum, **107**
Kane, Thomas L., 107

kayaking. *See* boating
Kensett, John Frederick, **53**
Keystone Theatre, 68-**9**
Kinzua Bridge, 98-**100**
Kinzua Bridge State Park, 92-**3**, 98-101
Kinzua Dam, 108-9
Knox & Kane Railroad, **1**, **98-**9

Lackawanna Coal Mine, 49-**50**
Lackawanna County Mine Tour. *See*
  Lackawanna Coal Mine
Lackawanna Heritage Valley Authority, 41
Lackawanna Iron and Coal Company, 39
Lackawanna Station, **51**
Lackawaxen, 24-9
Lake Wallenpaupack, **13**, **30-**1
LaPorte House, 64-**6**
LaPorte, John, 64-5
Lawrence, 132-**5**
Leonard Harrison State Park, 79, **80-**1
Lichtenfels, Lisa, **136-**7
lighthouse, 125
Lincoln, Abraham, 15
Lind, Jenny, 67
Linesville Spillway, 117
Longhouse National Scenic Drive, 109
lumber industry, 24, 83, **84-**7
Luthers Mills, 70

Mansfield University, **74**
Marie Antoinette, 65-6
Marienville, 101
McDade Park, 46-50
McKean County Historical Society, **96**
Meadville, 120-1
Meadville Market House, **120-**1
Methodist Episcopal Church, **70**
Milford, **13**, 15-19, 29
Moravians, 59, 92
Morris, Robert, 64-5
Mt. Jewett, 99, 107
Mt. Pisgah State Park, 70-**1**
museums, 15, 17, 26, 34, 40-2, 43-5,
  46-8, 52-3, 64-7, 68, 84-7, 98, 102,
  103-4, 105, 107, 129-35, 136
music festivals, 15, 35

National Engineering Landmark, 99
National Forest. *See* Allegheny

141

National Forest
National Historic Landmark, 18, 74
National Natural Landmark, 124
National Park Service, 25, 43
National Register of Historic
  Places, 70, 74, 122
Native Americans, 11, 17, 59, 60, 92, 122
natural history. *See* museums
New Process Company. *See*
  Blair Corporation
Niagara, 128-35, **130-1**
Nicholson, 56-7
Nicholson, John, 64-5
Nixon, E.L., 88
North Branch Canal, 63
North Country National Scenic
  Trail, 109

Oil industry, 102
outdoor recreation, 15, 22, 29, **30-1**, 35, 70, **76**-7, 78-9, **82-3**, 84-7, 88, **90-1**, **108-11**, 117, 123, 124, 128. *See also* boating

Packer Park, **77**
Penn, William, 31
Penn-Brad Oil Museum, 102
Pennsylvania Anthracite
  Heritage Museum, **46-8**
Pennsylvania Historical and Museum
  Commission, 4-**5**, 46, 66, 86, 129-32
Pennsylvania Lumber Museum, **84-87**
Pennsylvania Route 7. *See*
  U.S. Route 6
Pennsylvania State Forests, **83**, **90-1**, 92
Pennsylvania State Parks, 70-**1**, **76**-7, **78-81**, 86, 92-**3**, 98-101, 124-**7**
*Pennsylvania Tapestry:
  Scenes form the Air*, 108
Perry, Oliver Hazard, 128-34
Pierce, Charles Sanders, 17
Pike County Historical Society, 15
Pinchot, Cornelia (Bryce), 19-21
Pinchot, Gifford, 17-21
Pine Creek Gorge. *See* Grand
  Canyon of Pennsylvania
Potato City Country Inn, **88**
Potter County Historical Society, 92
Presque Isle Lighthouse, **125**, 128

Presque Isle State Park, 124-**7**, 134
Pymatuning Reservoir, 117-**9**

Rafting. *See* boating
railroads, 37, **43-5**, **51**, 56,
  62-3, 86-7, 98-**101**, 132
Reagan, Ronald, 104
reservoirs, 108-9, 117-**9**
Rigas, John, 92
rivers, **22-3**, 24-5, 54-**5**, 59, **62-4**
Riverside Inn and Hotel, **116**-7
Rockwell, Jarvis, 105
Roebling Bridge. *See* Delaware Aqueduct
Roebling, John Augustus, 24
Roosevelt Highway. *See* U.S. Route 6
Roosevelt, Theodore, 11
roundhouse, 44

St. Rose of Lima Church, 39
Scranton, 39-53
Scranton family, 39
Settlers Inn at Bingham Park, **33**
Shohola Recreation Area, **29**
Slate Run Village, 90
Smethport, **96-7**
spa, 117
State Forests. *See* Pennsylvania
  State Forests
State Parks. *See* Pennsylvania
  State Parks
Steamtown National Historic
  Site, **43-45**, 56
Stourbridge Lion, 37
Struthers Library Theater, **115**
Struthers, Thomas, 115
Struthers Wells Company, 115
Susquehanna River, 54-**5**, 59, **62-3**, 64
Susquehannock Trail, 90
Suydam, Fred, 35
Swedish Evangelical
  Lutheran Nebo Church, **106-7**

Theatres, 68-9, 86, 115
Thundercloud, Chief, 17
timber. *See* lumber industry
Torrey, Jason, 36
Towanda, 64-70
trolleys, 40-**2**
Troy, 70, 72, 74-**5**

142

Troy Half-Shire House. *See*
 Van Dyne Civic Building
Tunkhannock, **58**
Tunkhannock Viaduct, 56-7
Turkey Ranch, 79

Upper Delaware Scenic and
 Recreational River, **22-3**
U.S. Army Corps of Engineers, 109
USDA Forest Service, 17-9
U.S. Route 6, history of, 11
Van Dyne Civic Building, 74-**5**
viaducts. *See* bridges

War of 1812, 128-34
Warren, 112-5
Warren County Courthouse, 112-**3**
Warren, Joseph, 112
Waterford, 122
Wellsboro, **10**, **77**, 79
wetlands, 77, 118-9, 123
White Mills, 34-5
Wildflower Festival of Music & Art, 15
wildlife refuges, **14**-15, **35**, 120, 122-3
Wilson, James, 31
World War II, 103-4
Wyalusing, **59**-63
Wyalusing Rocks Overlook, **60-3**

Zane Grey Museum, 26, **27-8**
Zippo/Case Visitors Center, 103-4
Zippo lighters, 103-4

ROUTE 6 TOURIST ASSOCIATION AND CONVENTION AND VISITOR BUREAUS

PA Route 6 Tourist Association
35 Main Street • Galeton, PA 16922
(814) 435-7706/1-87-PAROUTE6
www.paroute6.com

Pocono Mountains Vacation Bureau
1004 Main Street • Stroudsburg, PA 18360
(570) 421-5791/1-800-POCONOS
www.800poconos.com

**Northeast Pennsylvania Convention
& Visitors Bureau**
99 Glenmaura National Blvd •
Scranton, PA 18507
(570) 963-6363/1-800-22-WELCOME
www.visitnepa.com

Endless Mountains Visitors Bureau
712 Route 6 East • Tunkhannock, PA 18657
(570) 836-5431/1-800-769-8999
www.endlessmountains.org

Tioga County Visitors Bureau
114 Main Street • Wellsboro, PA 16901
(570) 724-0635/1-888-TIOGA28
www.visittioga.com

Potter County Visitors Association
P.O. Box 245, Coudersport, PA 16915
(814) 435-2290/1-888-POTTER2
www.pottercountypa.org

Allegheny National Forest Vacation Bureau
80 E. Corydon Street • Bradford, PA 16701
(814) 368-9370/1-800-473-9370
www.allegheny-vacation.com

Northern Alleghenies Vacation Region
315 Second Avenue • Warren, PA 16365
(814) 726-1222/1-800-624-7802
www.northernalleghenies.com

**Crawford County Convention
& Visitors Bureau**
211 Chestnut Street • Meadville, PA 16335
(814) 333-1258/1-800-332-2338
www.visitcrawford.org

Erie Area Convention & Visitors Bureau
109 Boston Store Place • Erie, PA 16501
(814) 454-7191/1-800-524-ERIE
www.EriePA.com

Come, enjoy Pennsylvania.
{in your favorite armchair}

NEW RELEASES

PENNSYLVANIA HERITAGE: DIVERSITY IN ART, DANCE, FOOD, MUSIC, AND CUSTOMS: HC, 9" x 12", 180 PHOTOS, 160 PGS., **$32.00**

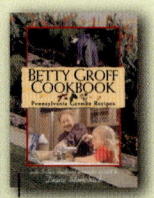

BETTY GROFF COOKBOOK: PENNSYLVANIA GERMAN RECIPES: HC, 7" x 10", 100 PHOTOS, 144 PGS., **$29.95**

WESTSYLVANIA HERITAGE TRAIL: A GUIDE TO SOUTHWEST PENNSYLVANIA'S HISTORIC PLACES: 6" x 8", 50 PHOTOS, 144 PGS., **$16.95**

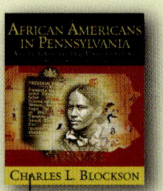

AFRICAN AMERICANS IN PENNSYLVANIA: ABOVE GROUND AND UNDERGROUND: BY CHARLES L. BLOCKSON, HC, 7 1/2" x 9", 140 HISTORIC PHOTOS, 320 PGS., **$29.95**

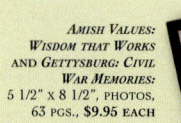

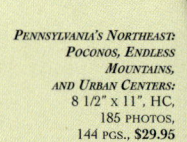

SUSQUEHANNA HEARTLAND: HC, 8 1/2" x 11", 200 PHOTOS, 144 PGS., **$29.95**

PENNSYLVANIA'S NATURAL BEAUTY: HC, 8 1/2" x 11", 120 PHOTOS, 120 PGS., **$24.95**

AMISH WAYS: HC, 8 1/2" x 11", 150 PHOTOS, 120 PGS., **$24.95**

SAVE OUR LAND; SAVE OUR TOWNS: BY TOM HYLTON, 8 1/2" x 11", 150 PHOTOS, 120 PGS., **$29.95**

AMISH VALUES: WISDOM THAT WORKS AND **GETTYSBURG: CIVIL WAR MEMORIES:** 5 1/2" x 8 1/2", PHOTOS, 63 PGS., **$9.95 EACH**

PENNSYLVANIA'S CAPITOL: HC, 8 1/2" x 11", 80 PHOTOS, 80 PGS., **$19.95**

PITTSBURGH: HC, 8 1/2" x 11", 125 PHOTOS, 128 PGS., **$29.95**

PENNSYLVANIA'S NORTHEAST: POCONOS, ENDLESS MOUNTAINS, AND URBAN CENTERS: 8 1/2" x 11", HC, 185 PHOTOS, 144 PGS., **$29.95**

PHILADELPHIA AND ITS COUNTRYSIDE: HC, 8 1/2" x 11", 180 PHOTOS, 144 PGS., **$29.95**

PENN STATE SPORTS STORIES AND MORE: BY MICKEY BERGSTEIN 300 PGS., 20 B&W PHOTOS, **$19.95**

PENNSYLVANIA'S TAPESTRY: SCENES FROM THE AIR: HC, 8 1/2" x 11", 90 PHOTOS, 96 PGS., **$24.95**

HARRISBURG: RENAISSANCE OF A CAPITAL CITY: 8 1/2" x 11", SOFT COVER, 238 PHOTOS, 144 PGS., **$29.95**

www.celebratePA.com
Featuring stunning color photos by Blair Seitz

AVAILABLE AT YOUR LOCAL BOOKSTORE OR AT SEITZ GALLERY
1010 NORTH 3RD STREET, HARRISBURG, PA 17102
CALL (800) 497-1427 FAX: (717) 238-3280